I dedicate this book to Maman.

Talat Yeganeh, my
grandmother

Ariana Bundy inherited her passion for food and cooking at an early age from her grandmother, 'Mamani'. She went on to become a French-trained chef, presenter and the author of _Sweet Alternative_, the first gluten-, dairy- and soy-free dessert cookbook. An Iranian-American, Ariana was Head Pastry Chef for the Mondrian Hotel in Los Angeles. She is a graduate of Le Cordon Bleu in Paris and also attended the European Business School in London, where she studied International Marketing and Finance. She has appeared on TV shows such as the BBC's _Good Food Live_, Sky's _Taste_ and _Top Billing_. Born in Iran and raised in London and New York, Ariana is fluent in English, Farsi and French. She now lives between Dubai and Paris with her husband Paul and their son Dara.

Pomegranates and Roses

First published in Great Britain by
Simon & Schuster UK Ltd, 2012
A CBS COMPANY

1 3 5 7 9 10 8 6 4 2

SIMON & SCHUSTER
ILLUSTRATED BOOKS
Simon & Schuster UK Ltd
222 Gray's Inn Road
London
WC1X 8HB

www.simonandschuster.co.uk

Simon & Schuster Australia, Sydney

Simon & Schuster India, New Delhi

Editorial director: Francine Lawrence
Project editor: Sharon Amos
Designer: Rashna Mody Clark
Food styling: Ariana Bundy
Photography: Lisa Linder
Props stylist: Mahshid Bazargani
Illustrator: Alice Chadwick
Production manager: Katherine Thornton
Commercial director: Ami Richards

A CIP catalogue record for this book is
available from the British Library

ISBN 978-0-85720-690-9

Printed and bound in China
Colour reproduction by Dot Gradations

Cook's Tips
Everyone in Iran has slightly different
ways of preparing the same dish. Over
time you will develop your own style,
especially in the use of fats, sugar, length
of cooking time and even how you prepare
vegetables. The ripeness of fruits and
using different cuts of meat all make a
difference to the end result too. Please
adjust the recipes to your liking.
Butter, oil, olive oil and ghee can be used
interchangeably unless stated.
Use a slotted spoon (flat and round is best)
when handling cooked rice.
Please use a Persian brand of
pomegranate molasses only.
All rice is basmati rice.
All recipes serve 4 unless otherwise stated.

Pomegranates and Roses

MY PERSIAN FAMILY RECIPES

ARIANA BUNDY

PHOTOGRAPHS BY LISA LINDER

SIMON & SCHUSTER ILLUSTRATED

London · New York · Sydney · Toronto · New Delhi

A CBS COMPANY

Contents

IRAN OR PERSIA?

Why are you so enchanted by this world
when a mine of gold lies within you?
Open your eyes and come~
Return to the root of the root of your own soul.

Rumi (13th-century Persian poet)

hile Persia conjures up images of nightingales, roses, poetry and gardens, Iran makes most Westerners uneasy. Growing up in Europe and America, my brother and I sometimes felt as though Iran was part of our imagination. Yet we knew it was real. We had tasted its food, climbed its hills and smelled its roses. We remembered the smell of the long-awaited rain when it first hit the dry earth; the first day of spring; the way the branches of the trees swayed before a storm and how the rays of the sun tried to pierce their thick leaves on Pahlavi Boulevard in Tehran; the colour and fragrance of my grandmother's roses. All these were real.

Yet Iran was never mentioned on the weather channel nor was it in the booklet of international dialling codes that was always next to the phone in hotel rooms. To us it seemed like the West was trying to sweep Iran under a giant (Persian) carpet. In school the textbooks didn't explain that Iran is modern-day Persia, instead making out Iran to be an evil country full of evil people with no culture or history. Even *Larousse Gastronomique* – the great cookery encyclopaedia – skipped Iran altogether, completely ignoring its culinary influence throughout the world.

With time, we also started to forget, thinking that our small family nucleus of four people was all we had left. Living in New York, a busy metropolis of people of all different nationalities and cultures, and where everyone was a stranger, the daily interaction and culture of the highly intricate *taarof* (a formal etiquette system) was gone.

The only time we would be drawn back to Iran was over a Persian meal, thanks to my mum, who would make time to cook us this elaborate food despite her hectic life. The smell of fried fish and dilled rice took me back to

Norooz (Persian New Year) parties at our grandparents' home. Memories would come flooding in over a bowl of Asheh Reshteh (New Year noodle soup, page 98) or Mast o Khiar (cold cucumber soup, page 136). Fried onions and fresh herbs brought back images of our housemaids sitting in the kitchen gossiping while we pulled at their skirts. Our American friends were so impressed when we ate these dishes. For them it was like an exotic feast.

We thought it was temporary, this being away from home bit. So we enjoyed ourselves, knowing that we would soon return. Yet every day we would watch the news and Iran seemed to be getting pulled deeper into darkness. Those were sombre days: watching our parents and grandparents worry for our country and loved ones; hearing news of our relatives losing their belongings or being stuck in the country when the Iran–Iraq war began. The war lasted eight years. But children are resilient, and we forgot and moved on with our daily lives. Except for moments when we did remember – and wished we were there in the comfort and love of the country we left behind. Those were confusing times – times when we didn't know who we were or how to explain to others what was happening to our country.

When I left home, I couldn't cook for myself. I would rely on eating as much as I could at those rare family gatherings. Persian food seemed so out of reach for me. Even after studying at Le Cordon Bleu and cooking for different establishments, I still wouldn't make Persian food. No one had taught me how! This is not something new. Many Iranians of my generation struggle with Persian dishes.

It wasn't until I was writing this book that I felt as though I was finally home. The research I did confirmed what I had always known in the back of my mind – even though I had been told otherwise – that Iran is a beautiful country with an amazingly rich culture. Its culinary heritage is incredibly varied and dates back thousands of years. Persia greatly influenced other cuisines around the world during its culinary renaissance. And in order to understand its future you must look back at its history. As the great innovative French chef Pierre Gagnaire has said, cooking should be 'looking towards the future but respectful of yesterday'.

For me, Iranian recipes are intertwined with its rich history, its people, and my ancestors. I gathered recipes by email, phone and by travelling: to Tehran, to the Caspian sea, to Ghazvin and remote villages – some people even parted with their old *nalbekis* (tea cups) and spoons so that I could take them home! I went to relatives' kitchens around the world, to London, Paris, LA, NY, Geneva. All this showed me that you can indeed make this fabulous food wherever you are.

Rolling my sleeves up in different kitchens, that's when it all came back to me. I say came back because I knew what everything tasted like. My taste memory hadn't failed me. I had been hungry for so long! Coupled with the fact that I am a trained chef, I was able to pick things up relatively quickly, as well as suggesting short cuts and slightly different ways of presenting this ancient cuisine – all the while staying true to its roots.

But most importantly, by learning about my family ties to the land, I was able to understand why I became a chef. It was this land of plenty that sustained the many generations of my family and made us appreciate the fruits and vegetables of our labour.

I hope you enjoy the recipes and stories that have made my life much richer as a result. From our land and our kitchens to yours!

> Persia greatly influenced other cuisines around the world during its culinary renaissance. And in order to understand its future you must look back at its history.

Clockwise from top right: my maternal grandparents, Talat and Akbar Bazargani; group picture, including Talat, Khaleh Eshrat and Khaleh Effat, and their little rascals; my mum's wedding day; my aunt and mum as children, dancing at a wedding; my grandmother's cousin (*left*), who taught table manners and etiquette to the Pahlavi royal family; my mum (*left*) with her brother and sister

POMEGRANATES AND ROSES, SAFFRON AND SPICES

land of four distinct seasons and varied landscapes, Iran has snow-capped mountains and lush forests, dry deserts, tropical waters and deep rivers, palm trees on the southern coast and cedars in the north.

Even though most of Iran receives very little rainfall and the country has a large central desert, it has successfully managed not only to grow food for its own needs but also for export, thanks to a system of ancient underground aqueducts called *qanats*, invented by the Persians 3,000 years ago. These systems supply water for 75 per cent of the country's farms and households.

Iran's rich soil produces some of the world's best fruits and vegetables, as diverse as sugar cane, saffron, olives, dates, citrus and cottonseed, to roses, tobacco, cherries, rice, tea, pistachios – and the tastiest pomegranates. Iran is the biggest producer in the world of stone fruits, berries, saffron, caviar and pistachios. Most crops are indigenous, except for rice and tea.

Food is central to the lives of Iranians in different ways: medicinal, cultural, philosophical and historical. The Zoroastrian religion has had a profound impact on Persian cuisine, from the festivities of *Norooz* (Persian New Year, see page 194) to wedding feasts; while the system of *Unani* – the balance of hot and cold ingredients (see page 16) – uses food in a medicinal context.

Food played a great role in the culture of ancient Persia. Many pre-Islamic dishes are still served today, along with the ancient seating hierarchy that takes into account old and young, guests powerful and weak. When Cyrus the Great, the founder of the Persian empire, came to power in the sixth century, he imposed racial, linguistic and religious equality, abolishing slavery and restoring all destroyed temples. His law of human rights set the tone for Iran being a multi-cultural nation: Muslims, Christians, Jews, Assyrians and Bahai faiths have been part of our history for centuries. And they all eat the same food and make the same recipes: Iranian cuisine.

Persia had long been known for its food and wine among the ancient Greeks and other conquerors. During the Arab invasion of the seventh century Persians really influenced the culinary cultures of its neighbours, through *Adabe Sofreh* – the etiquette of eating and table manners that was taken up throughout the Arab, Ottoman and Indian empires.

During the 15th and 16th centuries, male chefs of the royal courts began to compile Iranian haute-cuisine cookery books. As Bert Fragner wrote in his

> Food is central to the lives of Iranians in different ways: medicinal, cultural, philosophical and historical

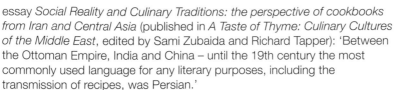

essay *Social Reality and Culinary Traditions: the perspective of cookbooks from Iran and Central Asia* (published in *A Taste of Thyme: Culinary Cultures of the Middle East*, edited by Sami Zubaida and Richard Tapper): 'Between the Ottoman Empire, India and China – until the 19th century the most commonly used language for any literary purposes, including the transmission of recipes, was Persian.'

And in the ancient poems of the *Shahnameh* or Book of Kings, right through to the poetry of Saadi, Hafez and Rumi, food played a central role and still does. All these factors intertwined at home with Persian hospitality, family customs and the tradition of *Nazri* – distributing food to the poor.

MEAT

Iranians are fond of meat, but in small quantities – except when they eat *kababs*. Either way, they like it meltingly tender. For *kababs* they marinate pieces of meat with lemon juice, saffron and yogurt then thread them on metal skewers (thin, thick or flat, depending on the cut of meat) and grill them on hot charcoal, while basting them with butter and more saffron.

Iranians also like to slow cook meat with fruits and vegetables, to create flavourful *khoreshts* (stews). Or they scatter it between layers of rice where it steams to perfection, flavouring the rice and creating a meal in itself. Iranian meat needs to cook for longer than Western meat, so it's best to keep an eye on it and check regularly for tenderness while following these recipes.

Meat is generally prepared using *halal* methods and, being an Islamic country, no pork is eaten – except by the Christian minority. The most popular red meat is lamb. Iran has a history of sheep breeding that dates back thousands of years. Today there are 27 breeds of domestic sheep and their most common characteristic is the long tail, which can weigh up to 10kg (22lb). The fat from the tail is called *dombeh* and it was used in the cooking of certain stews and pastries but less so now. The recipe for Ab Gousht (lamb shank soup, page 60) sometimes calls for *dombeh* if it is prepared traditionally. *Goosvand* (mutton) and *goosaleh* (spring lamb) are the favourite types, as they lend themselves especially well to stews.

Chicken and duck are often on the menu. Young chickens or *joojeh* (poussin) are especially popular for *kababs*. Duck is generally eaten in the Caspian region, while game birds are popular in the countryside.

RICE

Rice is taken very seriously. In fact you could say Iranians seem to have a love affair with it. Rice did not make an appearance in Persian cooking until relatively late in the eighth century. There is no word for rice in the Zoroastrian holy book *Avesta*, although some historians think rice was grown in Persia as early as the fourth century. The Persian word for rice, *berenj*, comes from the

Sanskrit, which suggests that it arrived via the Indian subcontinent.

The Caspian region is the main rice-growing area, where the climate is wet and humid. The people here consume large amounts of rice (even for breakfast) and rely very little on bread, whereas in the rest of the country people eat bread for breakfast, then rice for lunch and dinner.

Rice is the star of the table in Iran rather than a basic foodstuff. The grains must be kept whole, long and separated from each other, never soft and mushy. Different ways of cooking it include *kateh*, a compact dish made by cooking rice in water with butter or oil (page 109). *Polo* dishes require more preparation – soaking, boiling then steaming the rice (Polo Ba Taadig, page 106). In the 16th century around 70 recipes for *polo* were invented, including dishes studded with real jewels. Rice is also used for desserts, puddings, sweets such as *halva e tar* and cookies (Naan e Berenji, page 114). The age of rice is important. It needs to be stored for at least three to four months but is best eaten at around three years old.

DAIRY

Dairy plays a big role in Iranian cuisine. Fresh yogurts with different fat contents, soured yogurt, soured milk, *kashk* (dried fermented buttermilk; see page 144), feta, *panir-e-koozeyi* (feta that has been aged in terracotta pots; see page 130) and, recently, simple foreign cheeses such as Gouda, Cheddar and blue cheese are all eaten in great quantities. Feta cheese is the centrepiece of Noon Panir o Sabzi Khordan (a starter of bread, feta and herbs, page 132), its mild soft taste balanced by the sharp herbs.

Yogurt is used in marinades, salads and soups, and to create *taadig*, the irresistible crunchy golden rice that forms at the bottom of the pan when cooking Polo Ba Taadig (perfect fluffy rice, page 106).

Families go through tubs and tubs of yogurt. Even the smaller corner shops carry a wide range of natural yogurt such as low fat, full fat, extra creamy, strained (Greek), soured and so on. In the villages, soured yogurt is a favourite, with specks of soured cream interspersed in all that white creaminess. Noon o Mast, a simple combination of natural yogurt with some bread for dipping, is almost a national dish.

FISH

The Caspian sea is the largest landlocked lake in the world. Fishermen mainly catch sturgeon, sardines, bream, salmon, mullet, trout and the highly prized white fish *kutum* or Caspian roach (also known as *mahi sefid*). At the opposite end of the country, blue fin tuna and giant prawns are caught in the Persian Gulf. However, Iranians do not tend to eat much seafood due to the hot climate and, until relatively recently, the lack of refrigeration. So fish is on the menu mainly on the northern and southern coasts and in large cities.

SPICES

Iranians love spices and are proud of their light touch when using them, preferring to let the freshness and quality of the ingredients shine through. The use of spice is an art, a subtle sprinkling here and there to enhance, not mask. Soft delicate spices include cinnamon, cardamom, turmeric, cumin, coriander, *golpar* (hogweed powder), a little ginger, dried Omani lime powder and dried rose petals. They are added to stews, layered when steaming rice and added to pickles and jams.

Each household has its own way of adding spice and some even blend their own spice mix called *advieh* (see page 204). The king of all spices is saffron. Iran grows 93.7 per cent of the world's supply and it is the backbone of Iranian cooking. It is used in everything from rice and stews to desserts, cakes, sweets and even sprinkled in teas.

VEGETABLES

Whether mixed into stews, layered in rice, preserved in syrup or pickled – Iranian pickles are called *torshis* – vegetables play a role in most meals. Some are chopped into salads or mixed with yogurt to make dishes such as Booraniyeh Esfenaj (spinach and yogurt dip, page 94). Broad beans and beetroot are steamed and eaten on their own as snacks. Another snack is corn on the cob, grilled and charred, then dipped in salty water. In olden times vegetables such as potatoes and beetroot were thrown in the *tanoor* (clay oven) and cooked then eaten sprinkled with *golpar* (hogweed powder) or dotted with butter. Tomatoes, sweetcorn, and sunflower and olive oils are relatively 'new'. Although the Caspian region has always grown its own olives, they are not as abundantly used as they are in neighbouring Turkey.

FRUIT

Iranians pride themselves on being connoisseurs, especially of fruit. Any Iranian abroad can tell you where to find the best of anything in a new city and will shop in many different stores to be sure of buying the best fruits and vegetables. News of the arrival of the first oranges will spread through a neighbourhood like wildfire! Vendors by the sides of the roads sell mountains of strawberries or white mulberries or sour cherries.

Fruits are eaten seasonally, which goes hand in hand with the philosophy of *Unani* (see page 16). In recent times, watermelons have appeared on sale in winter, but people steer away from them, saying that they've been kept in *sard khooneh* (cold storage) from last year. Unripe fruits are also prized, such as green sour plums and unripe grapes – both are added to stews.

Iranians eat fruits whole as a snack or at the end of a meal – and almost always chilled. They also use them in desserts and to make conserves, which are sometimes served to end a heavy meal. Fruits are stuffed to make

dolmehs and added to thick hearty soups (*ash*) and stews to create that distinct Persian sweet and sour flavour. Dried fruits are added to *ajeel* (trail mix, page 68) and to rice dishes to counterbalance the richness of the meat.

Fruit juice stands are a familiar sight in towns and villages, offering a variety of freshly squeezed juices and fruit cocktails such as *ab e anar* (pomegranate) and *shir moz* (banana milk shake). Pomegranate juice is cooked down to thicken it, then dried to make a sour paste – vital for dishes like Khoresht Fesenjan (rich pomegranate and walnut stew, page 26).

TEA

Tea was not part of early Persian culture. In fact, coffee was the drink of choice until the first half of the 19th century. Then tea took the country by storm. Now almost every home in Iran has a samovar – an old Russian brass or modern metal kettle with a porcelain tea pot on top – boiling away, the tea steeping to perfection and ready to be drunk throughout the day. Iranians drink up to 10 *estekans* (tulip-shaped glasses that sit on a saucer) a day!

Tea is so engrained in Iranian households that children as young as two start drinking weak tea with their breakfast. It is never drunk with milk except on the border with Pakistan. Everywhere else tea is drunk plain, with a slice of dried lime, a pinch of saffron, some sugar or a squeeze of lemon. The Iranian way is to put hard sugar lumps (chipped from a large sugar loaf) or factory-made cubes on the tongue and then drink the tea. People either drink tea *por rang* or *kam rang* – light or dark.

NUTS AND PULSES

Iran produces a great variety of nuts, including almonds, walnuts and pistachios. Iranians eat nuts fresh or roasted, on their own or ground up to make sweetmeats, in stews and soups, pickled, caramelised or sugared. Pulses are also important and need to be cooked for longer than in the West. Chickpeas and lentils are used mainly in hearty soups but also in stews, rice dishes and even desserts and snacks.

GRAINS

Bread is served at almost every meal. As in France, fresh bread is bought every morning from the many local bakeries. Each specialises in one particular type of bread. *Barbari*, similar to focaccia but thinner, is crusty on the outside and fluffy on the inside and sprinkled with sesame seeds. It is usually eaten for breakfast. *Lavash* is normally eaten with meals, such as stews, but also with feta and herbs (page 132). *Sangak*, meaning stone bread, is cooked over small black pebbles in a hot oven. *Taftoon* is great as a breakfast bread. *Shirmal* is made with milk, like brioche.

UNANI
The Hot and the Cold

Unani, the system of 'hot and cold' humours used in Persian cooking, is not based on temperatures but on the principle of categorising foods – and people – into two main types. In a nutshell, all dishes should be a balance between the two and, if they are, people will stay healthy. Although it dates back centuries, it's something that everyone in Iran understands instinctively and practises in their everyday cooking and eating, even today.

The basic system of *Unani* was developed by the early Persian physician, scientist and philosopher Hakim Ibn Sina (also known as Avicenna). He was from Bukhara, part of the Persian Empire during Islam's Golden Age. His ground-breaking medicinal encyclopaedia, *The Canon of Medicine*, became a university text book and was studied in Europe right up until the 18th century, and is still used in *Unani* colleges and universities today.

Everyone in Iran is brought up to know which category their own body type leans towards and which foods fall into each category. So if someone has a cold constitution, they generally eat more hot foods to warm up their bodies, and vice versa. The local *attari* or herbalist also offers more advice. Mothers get to know their babies and feed them accordingly. Do they kick off the blanket, get spots when they eat nuts or have lots of tummy aches? Then they are hot babies and need cold foods.

Cold foods such as cucumbers, yogurt, watermelons and chicken tend to have less energy value, as opposed to hot foods like nuts and bananas. Items such as salt are considered neutral. 'Dry' and 'wet' humours also come into play – when a person is healthy, all four humours are balanced.

Here are some examples. Fesenjan (rich pomegranate and walnut stew, page 26) is a balance between pomegranates (cold) and walnuts (hot); it's almost always eaten in autumn or winter – eating it in the summer will make you 'burn'. Mast o Khiar (cold cucumber soup, page 136) is a balanced dish of hot and cold ingredients but tends to lean towards the cold, so it is served with hot foods such as Koreshteh Ab Ghooreh o Bademjoon (aubergine and tomato stew, page 48), but never with very cold items such as fish. Raisins and walnuts are hot. Dairy products and mint are cool and eaten in the summer. *Torshi* (pickles, page 84) are mainly cold because of their vinegar content, so are served as an accompaniment to hot foods – although if they contain garlic, they are classified as hot! (Turn the page to see how my grandmother grouped everyday foods.)

Each season has its own dishes. Spring dishes include Baghali Polo (dilled rice with broad beans and tender lamb, page 193); summer, Albaloo Polo (sour cherries with rice and meatballs, page 52); autumn, Khoresht Fesenjan (see above); winter, Halim (creamy lamb or turkey porridge, page 216).

A person's diet is also determined by where they live, not just because of regional availability of foods but also the climate. In the *Unani* system, garlic absorbs humidity and so it and spicier foods in general are eaten in hot and humid climates. Cooks also consider the person's age, their health, the time of the day, the season, and the occasion, when preparing a meal.

Everyone in Iran is brought up to know which category their own body type leans towards and which foods fall into each category

Pomegranates are cold foods

Garmi
(HOT)

apples
bananas
carrots
caviar
chicken
chickpeas
dates
duck
eggs
figs
garlic
herbs (except parsley and coriander)
lamb
nuts (any sort)
olives
onions
pears
pepper
quince
radishes
raisins
rose water
spices (all except sumac, but including saffron)
sturgeon
tea
turkey
vinegar
wheat
whey (*kashk*)

Clockwise from top left: tea; saffron-tinted rock candy; rose water; saffron; turmeric, cardamom and caraway; caviar

Sardi

(COLD)

all unripe fruits
apricot
aubergine
barberries
beef
beetroots
celery
cherries
citrus fruits
coffee
cucumbers
dairy products
(except whey)
fish (except sturgeon
and caviar)
grapes
green beans
lentils
lettuce
mulberries (black)
peaches
plums
pomegranates
potatoes
prunes
rice
rooster
sugar
sumac
turkey
veal
verjuice
watermelon

Clockwise from
top left: grapes;
watermelon; candy
floss; pomegranate;
coffee; Omani limes

میوه

CHAPTER ONE

FRUIT

Under the Pomegranate Tree

There's a pomegranate stand in virtually every neighbourhood in Tehran – our equivalent of Starbucks. The bright red fruits are piled high, with just a little window for the seller, who pokes his head out to serve you with fresh juices and pastes.

Pomegranate trees are spectacular. There was a beautiful one in our garden with perfectly balanced branches, spreading out like wings. We could see it from the living room, framed by the window like a beautiful painting. The tree changed dramatically through the seasons, from falling leaves, to snow-covered twigs, then dark pink blossoms and finally green and lush, dotted with crimson globes that dangled elegantly from its branches like earrings. On lazy summer afternoons we would sit in its shade, drinking hot fragrant tea and feeling the tree's presence as if it were one of our ancestors.

Once the fruits were perfectly ripe, women picked and juiced them, staining their fingers and clothes. The ruby-red liquid is packed with health-giving tannins and antioxidants; it was cooked over a slow fire until it formed a thick burgundy paste. Some pastes were sour, others sweeter, depending on the variety of pomegranate.

Some of this paste would be bottled for making the famous Khoresht Fesenjan (rich pomegranate and walnut stew, page 26) and Asheh Anar (pomegranate soup, page 32). The rest would be quickly spread while still hot on to clean plastic tablecloths using a circular motion, just like making a crepe. The cloths were taken up to the roof and anchored by bricks so that they would not be lost to the winds. Within days, the hot sun turned the pomegranate paste into sweet and sour leathery discs, which were rolled up, wrapped and stored, to be enjoyed throughout the year.

Pomegranates are indigenous to Iran and the Himalayas and have been cultivated there for about 4,000 years. Iran is the second biggest exporter in the world. As well as red, you can buy fruits with pink, yellow, brown and even black seeds.

In Persian mythology, pomegranates are associated with fertility, renewal and marriage. In Islam, they are symbols of God's abundance; in Christianity, paintings often depict Mary holding a pomegranate to symbolise the resurrection. In Judaism, the pomegranate is reputed to have 613 seeds, corresponding to the Torah's 613 commandments. Pomegranate trees in the courtyards of Iranian temples symbolise eternal life in the Zoroastrian religion, as their leaves remain green all year round.

In the doctrine of *Unani* medicine (page 16), the pomegranate is a 'cold' food used for balancing a 'hot humour'. Pomegranate teas combat many ailments, including nausea. The tannins are said to purify the blood and also to cut cholesterol.

As kids we used to gently roll the fruit on a table or hard surface. Then when all the seeds inside were crushed to a soft mush, we would bite a tiny piece off the top or side. By pressing on both sides of the fruit, we got a rush of sweet and sour juice. We kept at it until we were left with a deflated leathery ball, which we threw away.

FAMILY MEMOIR

Jelleye Anar
(see recipe overleaf)

JELLEYE ANAR
FRESH POMEGRANATE
JELLY WITH
POMEGRANATE SEEDS

2 sachets or 3 leaves
of gelatine

1.5 litres (2½ pints)
6 cups freshly squeezed
pomegranate juice
or shop-bought unsweetened juice
(such as Pom Wonderful)

1½ tbsp caster sugar
(optional)

500g (1lb) 3 cups
pomegranate seeds

gold leaf, to decorate (optional)

fresh rose petals, to decorate
(optional)

One of the first things my brother and I were allowed to make was jelly. We would mix the fresh pomegranate juice with powdered gelatine and crunchy seeds and get our fingers all red. We filled dessert glasses with the ruby liquid, placed them on a tray and ever so slowly put it in the fridge. But we never had the patience to let the jellies set, checking them at least ten times before devouring them semi-runny. This recipe is very far removed from the usual packet jelly but has the same texture. The jellies look absolutely stunning served in martini glasses or any other pretty glasses (see previous page).

In a large bowl, dissolve the powdered gelatine with 250ml (8fl oz) 1 cup of the pomegranate juice. If using gelatine leaves, place them one by one (not all at once or they will stick together) in a large bowl filled with cold water and leave for about 10 minutes. Once they are soft, gently pick them up and squeeze out any water with your hands.

On a low heat, warm up the rest of the juice in a saucepan then add the gelatine mixture or gelatine leaves and stir constantly until thickened. Taste the mixture and if it's too sour, add the sugar until you achieve the desired taste. Pour the jelly into a large glass bowl or small glasses, then sprinkle in the seeds, reserving a few to decorate.

Leave to cool before transferring to the fridge to set. Before serving, decorate the jelly with the rest of the pomegranate seeds; crumble over the gold leaf and scatter with fresh rose petals, if using.

KHORESHT FESENJAN
RICH POMEGRANATE AND WALNUT STEW WITH CHICKEN

250g (8oz) 4 cups ground walnuts

375ml (13fl oz) 1½ cups hot chicken stock or hot water

6 chicken breasts

3 tbsp olive oil

1 medium onion, diced

¼ tsp turmeric

¼ tsp white pepper

200ml (7fl oz) 1 cup freshly squeezed pomegranate juice or shop-bought unsweetened juice

3½ tbsp pomegranate molasses (Persian brand only)

1½ tsp brown sugar

4–5 x 10cm (4in) squares of *lavashak* (Persian fruit roll)

pinch of saffron threads, pounded then dissolved in 2 tbsp hot water

1 tsp sea salt, plus extra to taste

twist of pepper

fresh pomegranate seeds and gold leaf (optional), to serve

You know you are a special guest when your host serves you Fesenjan. It's a real treat, as it takes longer than most dishes to prepare. This medieval stew comes from the Caspian region of Iran. Traditionally, it was made with wild duck and scattered with small lamb meatballs. Now it's more commonly made with chicken. This is a perfect example of a hearty 'hot' dish (see *Unani*, page 16), served in autumn and winter. The pomegranate, a winter fruit, adds acidity to balance and bring all the flavours together. I've used chicken breasts to cut the cooking time and very little oil as walnuts are so rich in fatty oils. Jazz up the stew's murky brown colour by scattering it with ruby-red pomegranate seeds just before serving. You can have it with simple steamed basmati rice or smoked rice. I've even served it with very un-Iranian mashed potatoes.

Place the ground walnuts in a heavy saucepan and stir constantly over a medium heat until light and golden, about 5–7 minutes. Don't let them burn. Slightly lower the heat, add the chicken stock or hot water, cover and cook for about 20 minutes.

In a frying pan, sear the chicken breasts with the oil, onion, turmeric and pepper until just golden. Add to the walnut mixture, cover and cook for a further 30 minutes on the lowest setting. An old lady from a village in the Caspian region taught me to leave a wooden spoon in the pot so that it conducts the heat and doesn't allow the stew to catch at the bottom.

Add the pomegranate juice, molasses, sugar, *lavashak* if using, and cook for another 30 minutes with the lid on. Add the saffron liquid 10 minutes before the end. The sauce is ready when it's a lovely dark colour and the chicken is tender. Season with salt and pepper. The stew should be a perfect balance of sweet and sour. If it's too sweet, add a bit of lemon juice; if it's too sour, add a tad more sugar. Sprinkle with pomegranate seeds and gold leaf before serving.

TIP: If you can't buy *lavashak*, add 10 Persian golden dried plums or 2 extra tbsp pomegranate molasses sharpened with lemon juice. Substitute firm tofu, roasted aubergines, shiitake mushrooms or potatoes for the chicken, for a vegetarian alternative. Or make the sauce by itself to serve with turkey at Christmas: omit the chicken, sauté the walnuts with the onions and reduce the stock by half.

Come to the orchard in spring.
There is light and wine,
and sweethearts in the pomegranate flowers.
If you do not come, these do not matter.
If you do come, these do not matter.

Rumi (13th-century Persian poet)

زیتون پرورده

ZEYTOON PARVARDEH

SWEET AND SALTY
MARINATED OLIVES
IN POMEGRANATE
MOLASSES AND
CRUSHED WALNUTS

125g (4oz) 1 cup olives

2 tbsp pomegranate
molasses

3 tbsp crushed walnuts

1 tsp finely chopped mint
and Asian basil, mixed
together in equal amounts

1 tbsp extra-virgin olive oil

pomegranate seeds,
to serve

If you are an olive aficionado you will appreciate this original recipe. It's made with green Caspian olives, so look out for smaller, more compact varieties in the West, such as Picholine from the south of France or Spanish Manzanilla. Although traditionally made with unpitted olives, I use pitted ones as the stones can be hard to distinguish from the flesh once the olives have been marinated. Iranians add a special herb called *choochagh*, which is unavailable in the West, so I've devised a mint and basil substitute. Salty, rubbery olives with sweet and tangy pomegranate molasses and deep nutty rich crushed walnuts – fantastic!

Crush the olives ever so slightly with a stone or pestle and mortar so that the marinade can penetrate. Then simply mix all the ingredients together (except the pomegranate seeds) and allow to marinate for at least a day and up to a month in the fridge. Scatter with fresh pomegranate seeds before serving. Serve with toothpicks or very small aperitif spoons.

Appetisers or *mazzes*: sweet and salty
marinated olives, plus a dish of sour plums

ASHEH ANAR
POMEGRANATE SOUP WITH GREEN HERBS

This is one of my mum's best recipes. Her country house on the outskirts of Tehran is set on a mountaintop with views of the valley and river below and of the snowy-peaked mountains beyond. Although only 20 minutes from the capital, sheep and long-horned deer graze on the slopes, there are quails in the fields behind the house, and wolves and coyotes howl at night. When the house is covered in snow, my mum makes this hearty deep-green soup with lots of fresh herbs, split peas and small rich meatballs. We eat it sitting in front of her giant fireplace. Leave out the meatballs for a vegetarian version.

Place 2 litres (3½ pints) 8 cups of the stock or hot water in a large saucepan, add the split peas and bring to the boil; reduce to a medium heat and cook for a maximum of 15 minutes. You want the peas to be *al dente*. Skim off the foam with a spoon. Add the rice, bring to the boil, then cook on low for about 30 minutes.

Meanwhile, make the meatballs. Mix the ground beef or lamb with the onion, turmeric, salt and pepper. Knead by hand for 5 minutes then roll into balls smaller than a hazelnut in its shell and set aside.

Check whether the rice and pea mixture has produced a creamy liquid – in Persian *La Ab Endakhteh*. When it has, add the chopped herbs and the remaining stock or hot water (you may not need it all), making sure it's boiling hot. Let the soup simmer on a low heat for another 30 minutes or so; leave a wooden spoon in the pan touching the base so that the soup doesn't burn at the bottom. It will look a bit volcanic at first as it bubbles up, with the chopped herbs refusing to blend in with the liquid. That's OK – they will eventually. Stir occasionally.

Sauté the onions in 1 tbsp oil until golden. Add the pomegranate juice and paste or molasses and heat through, then stir into the soup. Fry the dried mint in the remaining oil for a minute then stir in.

Either add the meatballs to the soup as they are or sear them first in 1 tbsp oil until brown on the outside but raw on the inside. This will give a richer taste; adding them straight to the soup will give it a fresher, healthier feel. Either way, once you've added the meatballs, season the soup, then cook for another 15–20 minutes or so.

To make the topping, fry the sliced onion in the oil until caramelised.

Once the soup is cooked, check the seasoning and balance it out by adding more molasses or lemon juice. Sprinkle with fresh pomegranate seeds and caramelised onions. Serve hot and enjoy!

For the soup:

3 litres (5 pints) 12 cups hot unsalted chicken stock or water

250g (8oz) ½ cup yellow split peas, soaked overnight

100g (3½oz) ½ cup rice

875g (1¾lb) 17 cups in total, of equal quantities of chopped parsley, coriander and spring onions or chives

2 large onions, sliced thinly

2 tbsp olive oil, plus extra

250ml (8fl oz) 1 cup freshly squeezed pomegranate juice or shop-bought unsweetened juice

75g (3oz) ⅓ cup pomegranate paste or molasses

1 tsp dried mint

2 tsp sea salt

pepper

lemon juice, to taste

For the meatballs:

500g (1lb) lean ground beef or lamb

1 medium onion, grated

½ tsp turmeric

1 tsp sea salt

¼ tsp pepper

1 tbsp oil, for frying (optional)

To serve:

1 medium onion, thinly sliced

2 tbsp olive oil

fresh pomegranate seeds (optional)

TASS KABAB E AREMANEH

AROMATIC LAMB CASSEROLE WITH TOMATOES, PRUNES AND CINNAMON

My mum makes the best Tass Kabab. I don't know what it is about hers. It is such a simple dish yet hers has all the juices and fragrance that can come out of cinnamon, meat, tomatoes and prunes. She would layer all the raw ingredients – including the meat, so no searing involved – then let it cook slowly while we did all sorts of things around the house. We knew the dish was done when the air was filled with the scent of caramelised onions, cinnamon and meat.

Tass Kabab is similar to a Moroccan tagine with its sweet and sour combination. Serve with crusty bread to soak up the juices left on your plate and some sharp *torshi* (pickles, page 84).

This recipe works best in a heavy cast-iron pot, but a regular casserole will do. Add 1 tbsp olive oil to the pan. Begin layering the ingredients. Start with the sliced onions: spread some out on the bottom of the pan. Then add a layer of meat, onions again, chopped garlic, carrots, potatoes and the tomatoes, sprinkling the layers with a little cinnamon powder, turmeric and salt and pepper and adding a few plums or prunes as you go.

Once all the ingredients are used up, add the rest of the oil, the butter and the lemon juice or powdered lime.

Cover, place on medium-high heat for about 5 minutes, then lower the heat to its lowest setting and let the casserole cook gently for about 45–60 minutes or until the meat is fork-tender. Add the saffron liquid 10 minutes before the end of cooking time.

I like to put the pot on the table and let everyone help themselves. Serve with some bread – and watch out for the plum stones!

TIP: If you don't have any plums or prunes or want to try a variation, substitute fresh apples or quince (with their skins on). Cut them into large chunks or wedges so they keep their shape while they cook. They will become soft, aromatic and add a sweet tang to the dish. You can also substitute 1½ tbsp green *advieh* mixture (page 204) for the individual spices.

---

2 tbsp olive oil

2 large onions, sliced in 1cm (½in) whole rings

1kg (2lb) de-boned leg of lamb or stewing beef, cut into 5-7.5cm (2-3in) cubes

3 garlic cloves, finely chopped

3 large carrots, peeled and cut into 5cm (2in) discs

3 medium potatoes, peeled and cut into 7.5cm (3in) pieces

4 tomatoes, sliced

1 tsp cinnamon

1 tsp turmeric

1½ tsp salt

few twists of pepper

10–12 Persian unpitted golden dried plums or pitted prunes

2 tbsp butter

juice of 1 small lemon or 1 rounded tsp powdered Omani lime (or more, to taste)

½ tsp saffron threads, pounded and dissolved in 2-3 tbsp hot water

KOOFTEH SABZI
MEATBALLS WITH RICE, HERBS AND PLUMS

There are different variants of *koofteh, kofta,* and so on, all over the Middle East. The name comes from the Persian verb *koobidan,* meaning to pound; they are meatballs made of rice and minced meat, herbs and spices, and stuffed with egg, walnuts or prunes. This recipe is from my lovely mum Mahshid, who told me a tip our cook Zahra Khanoom gave her: bark loudly '*Vagh!*' each time you slide a meatball into the broth. That way they get scared and hold themselves together and don't fall apart. She says this with a straight face and we can hear her loud and clear when she's in the kitchen cooking *koofteh.*

Fry the onion for the broth in the oil and butter until caramelised and a dark golden colour, but don't let it burn. Discard the oil and place the onions on a paper towel to absorb the remaining oil. Set aside.

Make the meatballs. Boil the soaked, drained split peas for about 15 minutes until soft but not mushy; add the drained rice to the water and boil for a further 5 minutes. Drain and cool.

Once the split peas and rice are cool, mix them with all the other ingredients and knead for about 10–15 minutes. In Persian this is called *Varz dadan.* (If you've asked your butcher to double mince the lamb, 5–7 minutes will do.) Or put the ingredients in a food processor fitted with a paddle or dough maker and put on low for about 5–7 minutes. Don't use a sharp blade otherwise the split peas and rice will get crushed. You need a soft smooth consistency that holds together.

Now form 8 tangerine-sized balls with the meat mixture. Flatten each slightly, with a hollow to hold the stuffing. Place a plum in each hollow. Wrap the meat mixture around them and roll into a ball again.

Meanwhile, heat 500–750ml (17fl oz–1¼ pints) 2–3 cups water in a pan large enough to hold the meatballs in a single layer and add the caramelised onion and a few plums. Bring it to a gentle simmer (not a rolling boil as the meatballs may fall apart in the liquid). Bark loudly – '*Vagh!*' – then gently lower the meatballs one by one into the pan. Cover and simmer on a low heat for 30–40 minutes. Add the verjuice 15 minutes before the end of cooking time. Gently roll the *koofteh* over about 3 times during the cooking. Lift the finished *koofteh* on to a dish, boil the broth for a few minutes then pour over the *koofteh.*

Serve with *torshi* (pickles, page 84) and some bread for dipping. Don't forget to warn your guests about the plum stones!

For the broth:

1 medium onion, sliced thinly

2 tbsp olive or safflower oil

1 tbsp butter

75ml (3fl oz) ⅓ cup verjuice or juice of ½ lemon

For the meatballs:

50g (2oz) ¼ cup yellow split peas, soaked for a few hours or overnight

125g (4oz) ½ cup rice, soaked for a few hours

500g (1lb) ground lamb (double minced if possible)

1 egg

50g (2oz) 1 cup coriander, finely chopped

50g (2oz) 1 cup parsley, finely chopped

25g (1oz) ½ cup garlic chives or spring onions, finely chopped

25g (1oz) ½ cup tarragon, finely chopped

15g (½oz) ⅓ cup summer savory (optional)

1 tsp salt

⅓ tsp black pepper

1 tsp turmeric

For the stuffing:

8 Persian unpitted golden dried plums, pre-soaked and soft or use pitted prunes, plus a few extra for the broth

My Grandfather's Land

My maternal grandparents, along with their brothers and sisters, owned around 40,000 acres of land near the town of Ghazvin, once the capital of Iran. On his land, Akbar Bazargani, my grandfather (or 'Baba'), grew wheat, barley, sugar beet, watermelons, apricots, apples, pears, cherries and alfalfa, as well as grapes – Ghazvin is known for having the best grapes in Iran. He also owned the villages on his land: picturesque clusters of mud and straw houses dotted in valleys and mountains.

My Russian-born grandfather and his four brothers were all landlords and merchants, like their father Haj Ali Asghar Tajeroff – the consul representing the Ottoman Emperor to the merchants of Ghazvin. Baba's eldest brother, however – my extraordinary great-uncle Sadegh – woke up one fine day and gave everything away to become a Sufi. He spent the rest of his life helping the sick and needy. And ever since he's been known as uncle Darvish (dervish) – an inspirational figure in our family.

Baba was the most amazing, lovable and down-to-earth person in the world, despite his wealth and influence. Big and robust, with a mane of white hair, he was loved by so many for his warmth, honesty and sense of fairness. He was a family man, who loved children, animals, the land, his farmers. He would go with his men and *monshi* (right-hand man), from village to village, over mountains and valleys for days on end in his Russian Pobeda (one of the first cars in Iran), or on horseback where he couldn't go by car, checking on the sheep, the crops and the people.

As a child I remember villagers unloading crates of juicy fruits and crunchy vegetables at our home in Tehran. I would watch as the women of the house descended on the produce. Some was washed and set aside for eating and cooking fresh, while the rest was made into preserves or pickled, or turned into pastes or vinegars for stews and marinades.

As a child
I remember
villagers
unloading crates
of juicy fruits
and crunchy
vegetables at our
home in Tehran

My aunt Maryam   My uncle Hormoz

Me

The resulting
jars, bottles and
containers were
all stacked in
our *sard khaneh*,
which was much
colder than the
rest of the
house because
of its extremely
thick walls –
almost like a
walk-in fridge

Fresh milk was churned into yogurt, butter, whey and cheese such as *panir-e-koozeyi* (aged cheese), for dishes such as Dolmage (page 130).

The resulting jars, bottles and containers were all stacked in our *sard khaneh* (chilled room), which was much colder than the rest of the house because of its extremely thick walls – almost like a walk-in fridge.

My grandmother told me that some homes in the 1920s and 1930s still had *sard khanehs* linked to the underground streams that irrigated much of Iran. Water flooded the room in the autumn; in winter it froze and, thanks to the thick walls, the ice would remain all year. It was used in drinks and to make ice creams, but most importantly, to keep food fresh.

Food was also stored in the *ambari* – a store room under the kitchen or in a separate building. It was an ideal place to keep grapes. They were hung from the ceiling, some for eating fresh and others to shrivel up and become plump raisins to use in *ajeel* (Persian trail mix, page 68) and in recipes such as Mast o Khiar (cold cucumber soup, page 134), Biscuiteh Keshmeshi (raisin cookies, page 45) and Adass Polo Ba Koofteh Ghelgheli (meatballs with lentilled rice, page 70), and also for snacking.

My grandmother made her own wine. Only the village children crushed the grapes with their feet – they were said to be cleaner than adults' feet! She also made verjuice, a sour juice pressed from unripe grapes, picked to thin out the crop, essential for the preparation of Persian *khoreshteh* (stews) and also for its medicinal properties (see *Unani*, page 16). The verjuice was also boiled down to make grape molasses. This luscious caramel-like syrup has a sour note at the end and is used to top rice pudding and in certain *torshis* (pickles).

Wine has enormous significance in Persian history. Its consumption dates back 7,000 years: archaeological remains unearthed near the Zagros mountains are said to be the first evidence of wine-making anywhere in the world. The main wine-producing districts were Shiraz, Hamdan, Isfahan and Ghazvin, and the importance of viticulture means that it did not disappear in Persia with the invasion of Islam.

My mother (Mahshid)

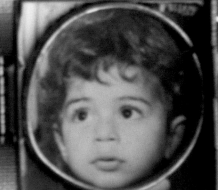
My brother Reza

My son Dara-Cyrus

مربای آلبالو سبک زهراخانم

MORABAYEH ALBALOO
SABKEH ZAHRA KHANOOM
ZAHRA KHANOOM'S SOUR CHERRY JAM

1kg (2lb) sour cherries,
pitted (if you can't find an
Iranian variety choose Morello,
Montmorency, or Early
Richmond cherries)

750g (1½lb) 3 cups sugar

Jam in Iran is normally eaten with bread and butter, or on its own with tea, but this goes just as well spooned over ice creams, rice puddings and other desserts. Sour cherry jam is fantastic with feta cheese. As a child, I used to drizzle the crimson jam over pure white feta and watch the colours mingle into fuchsia. My grandfather used to put a spoonful in his hot tea to give it a delightful fruity flavour, and my grandmother used to eat a few spoonfuls as a little something sweet after a heavy meal.

The recipe was given to me by Zahra Khanoom, our lovely cook who came to our home with her parents when she was only ten. Now 70, she is part of the family. She says that one way to know if the jam is ready (besides the plate test, see below) is when the bubbles get bigger and bigger, until they're the size of a *poolak* (sequin – about the size of a 10p piece).

Mix the cherries and sugar together in a large non-metallic bowl and let them sit for half a day or overnight in the fridge. This allows the flavours to combine and the cherries to release some of their juices.

Put the cherry and sugar mixture, including any juice produced, in a large preserving pan and place over a medium heat. Add up to 125ml (4fl oz) ½ cup water if it looks like the mixture is sticking. As soon as the mixture comes to the boil, reduce the heat to its lowest setting and let it cook for 30–45 minutes, skimming often.

While the jam is cooking, place a small plate in the freezer. After 20–30 minutes or so, put a small amount of jam on the plate, put it back in the freezer for 30 seconds, then nudge it with your finger. If it sticks and crinkles, it is ready to be potted up in sterilised jars.

Sour cherry jam and orange blossom preserve, with barberry jam in the background; recipes on pages 40–41

مربای بهار نارنج

MORABAYEH
BAHAR
NARENJ

HEADY ORANGE
BLOSSOM PRESERVE

fresh whole Seville orange
blossoms, enough to fill
1.5 litres (2½ pints) 5 cups
or the same volume of plain
orange blossoms or 50g (2oz)
2 cups dried petals

625g (1¼lb) 2¾ cups
preserving sugar

2 tbsp orange-blossom
water (if using dried petals)

1 tbsp lemon or lime juice

Preparing this preserve makes me feel like a fairy
princess brewing a powerful potion, with petals and
perfume everywhere! The kitchen is fragrant for
days afterwards. The fresh flowers are so heady my
grandmother used to tuck a few in her bra while cooking.

Iranians are famous for preserving everything from
fruits to vegetables. Originally made in the Caspian
region where the citrus trees grow, this is the perfect
example of Iranians using every part of a fruit – even the
petals. It isn't just a regular preserve with added orange-
blossom water: it's made from real flowers (although you
will need a dash of orange-blossom water if you use dried
petals). It is heady, sugary and translucent: the petals are
tender yet slightly crunchy. Eat it with ice cream, as a
topping on your favourite dessert, on its own with a glass
of tea or with bread and butter for breakfast.

Both fresh and dried petals need to be soaked in advance to remove
some bitterness as well as to soften them. Place them in a large
bowl and cover with cold water. Leave in the fridge overnight and
then drain, discarding the water. Alternatively boil the petals for about
10–15 minutes then strain.

In a preserving pan, make a syrup by boiling the sugar with 125ml
(4fl oz) ½ cup water for about 8–10 minutes on a low heat. Add the
orange blossoms and boil for another 20–30 minutes, then add the
orange-blossom water if using and lemon or lime juice, and boil for
another 2–3 minutes, skimming if you need to. Use the plate test
(page 38) to check whether it's ready. This jam isn't ideal for storing:
it needs to be kept in the fridge and eaten relatively quickly, otherwise
ice crystals may form. (Picture on page 39.)

MORABAYEH ZERESHK
TANGY BARBERRY JAM

I remember going on country walks in Iran and finding beautiful crimson barberries or *zereshk*, growing on sharp thorny bushes. They are sweet and tangy and Iranians love using them in jams, stews, and for stuffing meatballs and poultry. They are also considered to be a blood cleanser (see *Unani*, page 16) and they have been found to have antioxidant properties. I'm afraid that there isn't a substitute for them, but the good news is that the dried berries can be bought online or at Middle Eastern shops and kept in the freezer for a very long time.

This jam is high in malic acid, which gives it the wonderful tartness. It is gorgeous on bread and also as a little something sweet to eat with a glass of hot tea. The colour is so stunning you may just want to keep it on your dressing table instead of in the pantry!

275g (9oz) 3 cups dried barberries

675g (1lb 6oz) 3 cups sugar

2 tbsp lemon juice

Make sure you buy bright red dried barberries (avoid the dark dull berries). Start by cleaning them well. Pick out any stems, stones or other debris from the berries. The best way to do this is to tip the berries on to a large tray. Push them to one side then begin sifting through them one by one, moving the inspected berries to the other side. (My grandmother would give my grandfather this task when they were old.) Put the inspected berries in a colander or sieve, fill a large bowl with cold water (don't use hot as the berries will lose their colour and flavour) and place the sieve in the bowl for about 10–15 minutes.

Drain the berries and put them in a preserving pan with 1 litre (1¾ pints) 4 cups water and the sugar. Bring to the boil and boil for about 20 minutes on a medium to low heat. Skim and stir occasionally. Add the lemon juice and cook for another 30–35 minutes until a jam is formed. Use the plate test (page 38) to check whether it's ready. Pot the jam in sterilised jars. (Picture on page 39.)

زرشک پلو

ZERESHK POLO

RICE WITH TENDER CHICKEN, SAFFRON AND BARBERRIES

1kg (2lb) chicken breasts, with or without bones

½ celery stalk, chopped (optional)

1 large onion, finely chopped

2 garlic cloves, finely chopped

½ carrot, chopped

juice of ½ lemon

2 tbsp olive oil

50g (2oz) butter

1–1½ tsp salt, plus pepper

½ tsp turmeric

½ tsp saffron threads, pounded then dissolved in 2–3 tbsp hot water

For the rice:

prepare as for Polo Ba Taadig, see page 106

For the barberries:

75g (3oz) 1 cup dried barberries

1 tbsp butter

⅓ tsp saffron threads, pounded then dissolved in 2–3 tbsp hot water

3 tbsp sugar

When I have non-Iranian guests for dinner I've pulled out this recipe so often that my husband always knows what's on the menu! It's Iran's answer to chicken and rice: sweet and sour with juicy melt-in-the-mouth chicken, a lovely saffron-tinged *jus* with melted onions and butter, and ruby-red tart barberries studding the white fluffy steamed rice. It works every time. This is my quick version of the traditional method.

Preheat the oven to 180°C/350°F/Gas Mark 4. Place the chicken in a large bowl, along with the celery, onion, garlic, carrot, 250ml (8fl oz) 1 cup water or unsalted chicken stock (see Tip below), lemon juice, olive oil, butter, salt and pepper and turmeric. Mix until the meat is well coated. Transfer the lot to a heavy saucepan or ovenproof dish, cover and place in the oven for about 45–60 minutes.

Halfway through the cooking process, add the saffron liquid and stir the chicken mixture, so that everything is equally golden. Towards the end of cooking time, add a little more water or chicken stock if the liquid has evaporated. Leave the lid off for the last 10–15 minutes.

You can also cook the chicken on the stove if you prefer: follow the method for Khorakeh Morgh (chicken stew, page 58).

Cook the rice while the chicken is cooking.

Clean the barberries following the instructions on page 41.

Put the barberries, butter, saffron liquid and sugar in a pan. Cook gently on medium heat, stirring constantly, until the saffron water has evaporated and you smell a sugary, tart aroma and the berries are slightly caramelised. This will take about 5 minutes. They burn very quickly! Try adding 1 tbsp of chicken juices to plump up the berries.

I normally serve the chicken on a platter with all its juices, topped with some barberries, and serve the rice on the side and leave everyone to help themselves. Some people like to layer the chicken along with the barberries and the rice before serving.

TIP: Chicken breasts on the bone give a dish lots of flavour. If you have difficulty buying them, use boneless breasts and chicken stock instead of water, and reduce cooking time by a third.

Tangy barberries are used in sweet and savoury dishes

Jam session with Khaleh Eshrat

Khaleh (Auntie) Eshrat was my maternal grandmother's sister, the last of the old generation, who passed away two years ago. She was an amazing woman. Not particularly known for her beauty, as she was, in some ways, the ugly duckling compared to her two beautiful sisters. But she was very funny, a real flirt and an incredible cook. Her son Mehdi Hariri, a pharmacist, is convinced that given the chance, she could have been a botanist. He remembers taking her to a forest in Austria and she named the flowers and herbs and told him about their uses. She settled back in the town of Ghazvin after her husband passed away and all of her five children had left to build their own lives.

Khaleh Eshrat was a classic Iranian cook, making everything from scratch. Her jams would be stacked against the kitchen window with the rays of the sun shining through them like stained glass. Sour cherry, cucumber, pistachio, strawberries and pumpkin. I still have a jar of her aubergine pickle (Torshiyeh Liteh, page 187) and guard it with my life. 'Take, take, take!' she would say loudly – which brings me to her one and only fault: being too stubborn to wear a hearing aid. This made communication charming at times, but hair-pullingly frustrating at others. Especially when you were getting a recipe from her. Forget the fact that no one in Iran uses exact measurements. (One 'cup' in one house differs from a cup in the next house – an old tea cup is used as a standard.) The real problem started when she would turn away and not be able to lip-read you in the middle of making jam.

'The fruits need to be cut like this,' she would say, cutting the stems off the light yellow quinces. 'You add this much cardamom to your syrup, not more, it's not customary.' 'It's not customary where, Auntie?' 'Where? It's in the cupboard.' 'What's in the cupboard?' 'The sugar. It's in the cupboard.' 'Oh, OK. . .'

'Your syrup has to be thick before you remove the pan from the heat. Quick, get me the spatula!' 'Where is it, Auntie?' 'What?' 'Where is the spatula?' 'The spoon? No, I want the spatula! You cannot use a spoon, I tell you, it'll ruin it! I'll get it myself.'

We would then pour the hot fragrant sticky quinces, which by now had miraculously turned a beetroot red, into sterilised jars. Ten or twelve jars later, we would put the lids on tight and place them in her store room. The quinces become soft, delicate and fleshy with slightly chewy edges, giving way under the pressure of the knife to be spread on buttered fresh *barbari* bread.

Khaleh Eshrat was a classic Iranian cook, making everything from scratch. Her jams would be stacked against the kitchen window with the rays of the sun shining through them like stained glass

FAMILY
MEMOIR

BISCUITEH KESHMESHI
DELICATE RAISIN COOKIES

125g (4oz) unsalted butter, at room temperature

125g (4oz) ¾ cup icing sugar, sifted

2 organic eggs

½ tsp vanilla extract

tiniest pinch of sea salt

150g (5oz) 1 cup unbleached flour

75g (3oz) ½ cup raisins, washed

Iranians are mad about sweets! On Thursday afternoons pastry shops are filled with frenzied customers picking up orders for the weekend and taking home five, six, seven boxes of cookies, cakes and other delights.

The following is a classic cookie recipe that's been around since my grandmother's childhood. Before the revolution, my family used to grow grapes. One variety that we specialised in was the prized *Angoor yaghouti* or black Corinth grape, also known as the champagne grape. They are perfectly shaped miniature grapes that are seedless, compact, sweet, tight-skinned and super crunchy. The bunches are so tightly packed with berries that as kids we used to bite into them like whole fruits, pulling the stems out through our teeth and mouths. My grandmother made cookies when the grapes had shrivelled into raisins. In her recipe, nothing comes between you and the taste of the sweet chewy raisins. Use a small dark raisin such as Zante or Corinth, rather than the giant plump variety.

Beat the butter in a mixer or with the help of a hand-held whisk for a few seconds until fluffy. Add the icing sugar in three stages. The butter will now be light and fluffy.

In a separate bowl, whisk the eggs with the vanilla and salt.

Using the mixer or whisk, add the eggs to the butter mixture in stages. If you pour the eggs in too fast, the butter will look curdled and separate. If that happens, simply whisk it on very high speed for a few seconds until it becomes fluffy again.

With the help of a rubber spatula, gently fold in the flour in three stages, then add the raisins. Be sure not to overmix the mixture. Stop as soon as it has all been evenly incorporated. Refrigerate the dough for about 15–20 minutes.

Meanwhile preheat the oven to 200°C/400°F/Gas Mark 6. Cover a baking tray with parchment paper or line it with a Silpat non-stick baking mat. Drop small teaspoons of the dough on to the tray, leaving enough space in between them, and bake for about 8–10 minutes until golden around the edges.

دلمه برگ مو

DOLMEYEH BARGE MO
MOORISH STUFFED VINE LEAVES

Unlike Greek *dolma*, which are slightly sour and lemony, and have a fresher, 'less-cooked' taste to them, Iranian *dolmehs* are more decadent and rich. They have a hint of sweetness and are stuffed with rice, ground lamb and sometimes tart barberries or walnuts. Slow cooking makes the leaves a little sticky – really more-ish as well as Moorish. In season, the villagers would bring wooden crates of grapes to our home. The grapes nestled in between large beautiful leaves, which the cooks would snap off and make ready for *dolmehs*. The elaborate preparation and the quantity (usually a lot!) gave the ladies of the house an excuse to gather round to chat and gossip while stuffing and rolling the leaves like mini cigars. *Dolmehs* are usually served as an appetiser.

For the stuffing:

see Dolmeyeh Felfel
(stuffed peppers, page 152)

For the sauce:

see Dolmeyeh Felfel
(stuffed peppers, page 152)

50–60 vine leaves,
fresh or canned

olive oil, for oiling

lemon wedges, to serve

Prepare the stuffing and leave it to cool. Prepare either of the sauces.

If you are using fresh leaves, blanch them in batches of 3–4 in boiling water just for a minute or two. Remove them and pour some cold water over them. Let them dry. For canned leaves, drain off the brine, rinse them in cold water and set aside to dry.

Take a large wide pot or an ovenproof dish and oil the bottom well. Line the bottom of the pan or dish with leaves: use about three layers.

Now take some more leaves and clip the stalks with a sharp knife or scissors. Stack the leaves, vein side up (the presentation side needs to be smooth). Take a leaf and add one rounded tbsp of the stuffing. Roll slightly, then fold both sides in and continue rolling until you have a fat 'cigar'. If the leaves are small, overlap them so that you can wrap the stuffing comfortably. Place them in the pot or dish you prepared, laying them with the flap facing down. Lay them on top of each other as they start to fill the pan, packing them together snugly so that they don't fall apart during cooking.

Pour the sauce over the *dolmehs* and place a smaller ovenproof dish on top so that the weight keeps them from expanding and falling apart. Cover the dish and either place it in the oven at 180°C/350°F/ Gas Mark 4 for 1½ hours; or cook on top of the stove on a medium-low heat for about an hour or until the leaves are tender.

Arrange the *dolmehs* on a serving dish, spooning over some of the sauce to make them look glossy. Serve with the rest of the sauce on the side, plus lemon wedges.

KORESHTEH
AB GHOOREH
O BADEMJOON

AUBERGINE AND TOMATO STEW WITH TART GREEN GRAPES

10 small aubergines or 4 medium aubergines

4–5 tbsp oil

2 large onions, sliced thinly

500g (1lb) lamb or stewing beef, cubed, or 1kg (2lb) chicken breasts on the bone (see page 42)

few extra meat bones

3 garlic cloves, minced

juice of 1 lemon

1 tsp turmeric

400g can chopped tomatoes

500ml (17fl oz) 2 cups hot water or unsalted chicken stock

4–5 cinnamon sticks

1 tsp salt

few twists of pepper

1 tbsp tomato purée

4 medium tomatoes, halved

½ tbsp butter

125g (4oz) 1 cup unripe grapes or few tbsp verjuice

⅓ tsp saffron threads, pounded then dissolved in 2–3 tbsp hot water

The aubergine came to ancient Persia via India and, according to medieval Iranian writers of medicine, it needs to be cooked and eaten with caution as it causes a lot of 'heat' in the body (see *Unani*, page 16). In this dish, the sourness from the unripe grapes counterbalances the 'hotness' of the aubergines. The sour grapes occasionally pop in your mouth, filling it with an incredible tart flavour that cuts through the rich aubergines and tender meat. If you come across a Middle Eastern or Persian food shop during 'young grape' season, please make this dish with unripe green grapes. Frozen unripe grapes are equally good, or try canned. But if you can't find either, it is also fabulous with verjuice, which seems to be all the rage. Serve the stew with rice (*polo*, page 106 or *kateh*, page 109) and a bowl of fresh herbs (*sabzi khordan*, page 132).

Remove the bitter taste of the aubergines by cutting them in half, scoring them and sprinkling with salt. Place in a sieve and leave for about 30 minutes. This also draws out some of the moisture so the aubergines become firmer and don't soak up so much oil. Remove the excess salt with a paper towel. Dry them well before frying.

In a large frying pan, fry the aubergines on both sides in 3 tbsp oil on a low heat until golden brown. Remove to a plate lined with paper towels. In the same pan, sauté the onions in 1 tbsp oil; add the meat and the extra bones until well seared and browned. Stir in the garlic and cook for a minute or so. Add the lemon juice and let it sizzle. Add the turmeric and canned tomatoes and stir briefly. Add hot water or unsalted chicken stock to cover – but no more than 500ml (17fl oz) 2 cups. Place the cinnamon sticks on top. Cover the stew and simmer for about 30–40 minutes.

Remove the extra bones from the stew. Season with 1 tsp salt, pepper and add the tomato purée. Place the aubergines on the top of the stew, cover and cook for another 30 minutes.

Meanwhile, fry the fresh tomatoes on a high heat with ½ tbsp oil and the butter, for 30 seconds on each side just to give them some colour. Place them on top of the aubergines, scatter the grapes on top (or stir in the verjuice 1 tablespoon at a time, tasting after each addition), pour in the saffron liquid, cover and cook for another 20 minutes until the aubergines, tomatoes and meat are meltingly tender.

شربت آلبالو

SHARBAT-E-ALBALOO
SOUR CHERRY SYRUP

1.5kg (3lb) fresh or frozen
sour cherries, pitted
(if you can't find an Iranian variety
choose Morello, Montmorency, or
Early Richmond cherries) or use
900ml (1½ pints) unsweetened
sour cherry juice

1.3kg (2½lb) 5 cups sugar

When I think of this recipe I picture tall glasses of pink liquid and ice. Each guest is given a long-stemmed spoon to stir the drink as the syrup, being heavier than water, settles at the bottom and creates a layered look – deep red, then pink and finally light pink. Elaborately carved spoons were used in ancient times (there's one on display in the Victoria & Albert Museum in London). Different flavours of *sharbat* (sherbet), from lemon (*ab-limoo*) to mint (*nanaa*, page 190) and rhubarb (*rivas*), came into existence because Persians had to find a substitute for wine following the invasion of Islam. They came to be known as *sharbat* from the Arabic word *sharab* (drink).

Did you know punch originates from the Persian *panj* or five – a combination of rose water, lemon juice, sugar, grape juice and ice? Portuguese traders brought the drink to Europe and substituted rum for the grape juice.

In Iran all drinks are cooled with ice, summer or winter. In ancient Persia ice was brought from the mountains and kept in thick-walled underground storage rooms. The ice was shaved and added to *sharbats* to create frozen concoctions served at the tables of the wealthy.

Juice the cherries in a juicer and pour into a preserving pan. Add the sugar and 1.3 litres (2¼ pints) 5½ cups water and boil on a medium-high heat for about 10–12 minutes. Stir once in a while until the liquid becomes syrup-like. If you haven't got a juicer, you can boil the pitted cherries with the sugar and water then strain through a muslin cloth or jelly bag, but I find that too labour intensive.

Remove from the heat and cool before using or storing in sterilised bottles. Usually Iranians like to mix the syrup with 2 parts water to 1 part syrup, but you can mix it to your own taste. Drink with lots of ice.

Cherries are always served chilled for a refreshing snack (*above*); if you can find
dark sour cherries they make a delicious syrup (*left*)

ALBALOO POLO

SOUR CHERRIES WITH RICE AND MEATBALLS

500g (1lb) 1½ cups fresh or frozen sour cherries, pitted (or use Morello, Montmorency, or Early Richmond cherries)

200–250g (7–8oz) ¾–1 cup sugar, depending on taste

800g (1lb 10oz) 4 cups rice

1½–2 tbsp butter

few twists of pepper

1 tbsp cinnamon

For the taadig:

50–75g (2–3oz) ¼–⅓ cup melted butter, ghee or safflower oil, plus 1 tbsp for topping

1½ tbsp natural yogurt

¼ tsp saffron threads, pounded

For the meatballs:

1 small onion, grated, liquid drained off

1 garlic clove, diced

½ tsp salt, plus pepper

½ tsp turmeric

250g (8oz) ground beef

2 tbsp olive oil

You know it's *albaloo* season when you see small crimson cherries dangling from the trees in the countryside. As children, for us that meant red-stained fingers and a tummy ache. There's something highly addictive about that sour hit: we used to sprinkle the cherries with salt or, worse, with citric acid powder to make them extra sour! Albaloo Polo is a combination of small meatballs, plump cooked sour cherries and rice tinged slightly pink from their juice. The *taadig* (crunchy rice at the bottom of the pot) burns a little because of the sugar, creating a super-crunchy charred crust that people duel over.

Place the cherries and sugar in a bowl, and leave for an hour. Prepare the rice according to the method for Polo Ba Taadig (perfect fluffy rice, page 106), up to draining and cooling.

Place the cherry and sugar mixture in a saucepan and cook gently for 10–15 minutes. Add 1½–2 tbsp butter, a few twists of pepper and stir gently so as not to crush the fruit. Set aside and leave to cool.

Add the melted butter, ghee or oil to a heavy non-stick pan and heat briskly with 75ml (3fl oz) ⅓ cup water, the yogurt, saffron and 2–3 ladles of rice. Stir well and spread the mixture over the base of the pan and start layering the rice and sour cherries on top, rice first. Add the cherries using a slotted spoon – leave the juice in the pan – sprinkling a little cinnamon between layers. Shape the layers into a pyramid. Continue until the pan is almost full; leave a little room as the rice expands while steaming. Pour the cherry juice on top. (If you have any rice and cherries left over, make a mini pot for yourself or freeze them.) Cook the rice following the method for Polo Ba Taadig.

While the rice is cooking, make the meatballs. Knead the grated onion, garlic, salt, pepper and turmeric into the meat for about 5 minutes until paste-like. Form into small hazelnut-sized balls. Heat a shallow pan, add the olive oil and fry the meatballs on a medium-high heat on one side without disturbing, for about 2 minutes or until golden. Turn them over and fry the other side for another 2–3 minutes.

Once the rice has finished cooking, add a pinch of cinnamon to the top, cover and allow to sit for a further 2 minutes. To serve, layer the rice and meatballs on a platter, reserving most of them to go on top.

TIP: You can make this recipe using Zahra Khanoom's sour cherry jam (page 38) instead of fresh fruit. And serve chicken instead of meatballs – follow the recipe on page 58.

اشکنه آلبالو

ESHGENEYEH ALBALOO
EGG-DROP SOUP WITH
SOUR CHERRIES AND MINT

1 large white onion, thinly sliced

2 tbsp safflower oil

1 tsp butter

1 tbsp plain flour or rice flour

6–7 mint leaves, washed, plus extra to serve

1 tsp dried mint

salt, to taste

white pepper

1 litre (1¾ pints) 4 cups water or unsalted chicken stock

250g (8oz) pitted fresh or frozen sour cherries (if you can't find an Iranian variety choose Morello, Montmorency, or Early Richmond cherries), or use 50g (2oz) dried sour cherries (soaked for at least 6–8 hours in water)

2 eggs

This medieval soup is named after the Ashkanians; they ate it before combat to give them strength and power. It is super-easy to make and is something between a French onion soup and Chinese egg drop soup. This fruit version was given to me by my auntie Vida Shahroudy. She first made it on a camping trip to the swampy Caspian region with friends, when she was a young woman. They poked their heads out of their tents one morning only to find themselves surrounded by thick fog. They could hear the bells of the sheep grazing nearby and water flowing, but all they could think about was how hungry they were. They had staples such as onions, sugar, salt, flour, eggs, oil but not much else. My aunt picked some sour cherries and wild mint, and to everyone's surprise she cooked this lovely hot Eshgeneyeh soup within minutes. Serve hot, or cold as a refreshing starter.

In a saucepan, sauté the onion on a medium-high heat in the oil and butter, making sure they are golden not dark brown. Add the flour and stir for a minute or two. Add the fresh and dried mint, salt and pepper, and the water or stock and the cherries. Cover and let the mixture bubble away for about 15–20 minutes on a very low heat.

Crack the eggs in the soup and stir briskly but be careful not to crush the cherries. Stir for about a minute and pour into a serving bowl. Adjust the seasoning and decorate with a few mint leaves.

SHIRIN POLO

SWEET RICE
STUDDED WITH
ORANGE PEEL,
JULIENNE CARROTS
AND NUTS

This is the mother of all Iranian rice dishes, created around the 16th century under the reign of Shah Abbas. A similar dish – jewelled rice – was served at weddings and on special occasions in ancient times, when real gems such as rubies and emeralds would be used to decorate it. Serve with Khorakeh Morgh (chicken stew, page 58).

800g (1lb 10oz) 4 cups rice

peel of 2 large oranges, or 150g (5oz) 1½ cups ready-prepared peel

10 medium-sized carrots, cut into julienne strips

50g (2oz) butter

250g (8oz) 1 cup sugar

50ml (2fl oz) ¼ cup rose water

1½ tbsp cinnamon

For the taadig:

50–75g (2–3oz) ¼–⅓ cup melted butter, ghee or safflower oil, plus 1 tbsp extra for topping

1½ tbsp natural yogurt

¼ tsp saffron threads, pounded

To serve:

1 generous tbsp slivered almonds

1 generous tbsp slivered pistachios

Prepare the rice according to the method for Polo Ba Taadig (perfect fluffy rice, page 106), up to draining and cooling.

Place the fresh or ready-prepared orange peel in a pan and cover with water. Bring to the boil and boil for about 2–3 minutes, then discard the water. Do this 3 times to remove the bitterness.

Put 500ml (17fl oz) 2 cups water in a pan and add the orange peel, carrots, butter and sugar. Bring to the boil and boil for 15 minutes. Remove from the heat and add the rose water, then set aside.

Add the melted butter, ghee or oil to a heavy non-stick pan and heat briskly with 75ml (3fl oz) ⅓ cup water, the yogurt, saffron and 2–3 ladles of rice. Stir well and spread the mixture over the base of the pan and start layering the rice and carrot mixture on top. Start with a layer of rice. Then add a layer of the carrot and orange peel mixture, and sprinkle with 1 tsp cinnamon. Repeat the layers, making the rice into a pyramid shape.

Cook the pyramid of rice following the Polo Ba Taadig recipe again.

Now, in order for the almonds 'not to be too tough on the teeth' as the Iranians say, you can steam them on top of the rice. Add them about 5–7 minutes before you're about to take the rice off the heat. If you prefer, put them in a little china ramekin and place it directly on the mound of rice. Pistachios don't need this treatment as they have a more delicate texture and are best when they are a little crunchy. Serve the rice on a platter with Khorakeh Morgh and scattered with the almonds and pistachios.

خوراک مرغ

KHORAKEH MORGH
CHICKEN STEW

2 tbsp butter

1 tbsp oil

2 medium onions,
sliced thinly or finely chopped

4 large chicken breasts
or thighs, skinless, with or
without bones

1 tsp salt

twist of pepper

⅓ tsp saffron threads,
pounded then dissolved in 2–3
tbsp hot water

This little recipe will change the way you look at chicken forever. It is unbelievably simple and efficient: you will turn to it again and again, even when making dishes from other cuisines (I use it for Japanese hot pots, curries and cassoulets). It's a master recipe. All you need to do is put the lot in a pan and let the whole thing gently cook away. The trick is to check your chicken for tenderness around the 45-minute mark if it is boneless, and about an hour if it isn't. Depending on the thickness of your pan and the power of your stove, cooking times vary. If you miss the 'tenderness' point, your chicken will start to overcook and become dry. Once you get the hang of this, you will have tender fragrant chicken every time.

Put a large saucepan over a medium-high heat and add the butter, oil, onions, chicken breasts, salt and pepper. As soon as everything heats up – about 5–7 minutes – reduce the heat to its lowest possible setting. Cover the chicken mixture and let it cook ever so gently for about 1½ hours. Turn the chicken over halfway during the cooking process.

   When the meat is meltingly tender, add the saffron liquid, cook for a further 2 minutes, making sure the chicken is well coated with the saffron, and remove from the heat. Either layer the chicken with Shirin Polo (sweet rice, page 56) or serve them side by side.

آبگوشت/دیزی

AB GOUSHT

LAMB SHANK SOUP
WITH OMANI LIMES,
CHICKPEAS AND
SAFFRON

500g (1lb) lamb shank

1 medium onion, quartered

2 medium tomatoes,
skinned and quartered

1 tbsp tomato purée

125g (4oz) ½ cup dried
white beans (chitti or borlotti),
soaked overnight

75g (3oz) ⅓ cup chickpeas,
soaked overnight

1 tsp turmeric

3–4 small dried Omani
limes, pierced several times with
the tip of a knife

1 very large potato,
skinned and cut into 10cm
(4in) pieces

⅓ tsp saffron threads,
pounded then dissolved in
2–3 tbsp hot water

1–1½ tsp salt

few twists of pepper

This simple dish is a filling treat: when I know I'm going to cook it, I start eating less beforehand so I can really stuff myself! A typical dish in roadside cafes, the lamb shank is slowly cooked in a broth of dried limes, saffron, onions, chickpeas, tomatoes, white beans and potatoes. The broth is then strained and the solids are mashed together, meat and all, into a paste similar to French rillete. It is served with *sangak* bread and Sabzi Khordan (fresh herbs, page 132), and must be eaten in a specific way. Spread the bread with the mashed mixture, take a bite and sip a spoonful of the hot golden broth at the same time. Then cleanse the palate with a bunch of herbs and *torshi* (pickles, page 84) after every bite. *Dizi* restaurants in Tehran serve only this dish and each diner has their own individual copper pot of soup.

This dish can bubble away unattended, so there's no need to hang around in the kitchen. Take a big enough pot and add the meat with enough water to cover. Bring to the boil, then skim several times. Add the onion, tomatoes, tomato purée, dried beans, chickpeas, turmeric and 1.2 litres (2 pints) 5 cups of water. Simmer for 30 minutes then add the limes. Bring to the boil, then lower the heat and simmer for 2 hours. Add the potato and saffron liquid, and cook for another 30 minutes. Adjust the seasoning and set aside to cool a little.

Pour the soup through a sieve into a bowl. The meat and bones may have deliciously fallen apart by now. Remove the bones but don't throw them away. Spoon out all the potato and a few chickpeas, to add to the clear soup before serving.

This next step is optional but it will make your rillete a little more refined. Separate out the rest of the chickpeas and remove their skins; simply roll them between your fingers and the skins will easily peel off. Now mash all the ingredients (except the reserved potato and chickpeas) with a potato masher – or use a pestle and mortar as they do in *Dizi* restaurants. I don't use the food processor to do this, as the texture becomes stretchy. Mash until you get a rough paste.

Put the paste in a serving dish. Reheat the broth with the reserved potatoes and chickpeas, then serve in either a large tureen or in individual dishes. Remove the marrow from the bones and give it to whoever wants to eat it – my mother loves it!

If you have one, a pressure cooker is ideal for this recipe – it will cut the cooking time in half.

KHORESHTEH MORGH VA PORTEGHAL
CHICKEN WITH ORANGES AND SAFFRON

300g (10oz) 1½ cups fresh orange peel or 125g (4oz) 1 cup ready-prepared orange peel

4 large chicken breasts, cut into 5–7.5cm (2–3in) strips or 1 young chicken or poussin

1 tbsp olive oil

2 tbsp butter (optional – you can replace this with olive oil), plus a knob of butter (also optional)

1 large onion, sliced thinly

2 large carrots, cut into julienne strips but fairly thick

½ tsp turmeric

1 tsp cinnamon (optional)

juice of 2 large oranges or 350ml (12fl oz) 1½ cups fresh orange juice

juice of 1 lime or 1 small lemon

2 tbsp verjuice or white wine vinegar

1½ tsp salt

⅓ tsp white pepper

½ tsp saffron threads, pounded then dissolved in 2–3 tbsp hot water

2 oranges, cut into segments, keeping 4–5 pieces for decoration

1 tbsp slivered almonds

½ tbsp slivered pistachios, to serve

Porteghal is Persian for Portugal, but it is also the word for orange, because the early Portuguese traders brought this sweet fruit to Iran. However, Persians had their own indigenous citrus fruit, the *narenj*, but it's a sour orange. Arab conquerors took it to Spain where it is called *naranja* – you will know it as the Seville orange. In Iran it is used instead of lemon to squeeze over fish.

This recipe uses sweet oranges counterbalanced with lemon or lime juice since *narenj* are hard to find outside Iran. It is the Persian counterpart to duck à l'orange or Chinese chicken and orange stir fry. Adding orange peel and saffron makes it an aromatic and elegant dish.

Remove the bitterness from the orange peel by placing it in a saucepan filled with water and boiling for about 3–4 minutes. Drain off and discard the liquid. Repeat three or four times more. Do this whether you are using fresh or ready-prepared peel.

Meanwhile, in another large saucepan, cook the chicken with the oil, butter, onion, carrots, turmeric, orange peel, cinnamon if using, orange and lime juice, verjuice or vinegar, salt and pepper. Follow the method for Khorakeh Morgh (chicken stew, page 58).

Add the saffron liquid, orange segments, the almonds and a small knob of butter (optional, just to make the sauce a little glossier) and cook for another 5–10 minutes, trying not to crush the fruit too much, although inevitably some will melt into the sauce. Transfer the chicken to a serving plate, sprinkle with the pistachios and reserved orange segments and serve with rice (*polo*, page 106 or *kateh*, page 109).

Rich golden saffron liquid

آجیل و حبوبات

CHAPTER TWO
NUTS
AND PULSES

KHORESHTEH CHAGHALEH BADOOM

YOUNG ALMOND AND LAMB OR
CHICKEN RAGOUT

1 large onion

1 celery stalk (optional)

2 tbsp olive oil

2 tbsp butter

500g (1lb) green unripe almonds, young tender ones

150g (5oz) 3 cups fresh flat-leaf parsley, finely chopped

25g (1oz) ½ cup fresh mint, finely chopped

1 tbsp sugar

½ tsp tomato purée

250ml (8fl oz) 1 cup unsalted chicken stock or water

½ tsp dried mint

125ml (4fl oz) ½ cup fresh lemon juice or 75ml (3fl oz) ⅓ cup lime juice

½ tsp salt

½ tsp white pepper

1kg (2lb) chicken pieces on the bone or 1kg (2lb) de-boned leg of lamb or 1kg (2lb) stewing beef, cut into 5–8cm (2–3in) cubes

½ tsp turmeric

½ tsp saffron threads, pounded then dissolved in 2 tbsp hot water

Green almonds are sold by street vendors in Iran once a year. They stand on the street with their trolleys piled high with unripe nuts, which they sell in paper bags with a helping of coarse salt. As children, we used to shake the bags so that the sour almonds were all evenly coated with salt and devour them until we got stomach aches. When you bite into their delicate fuzzy skin, they make the biggest crunchy sound – they are so juicy and fresh on the inside. This stew can only be made for a limited time each year, so if you see fresh almonds displayed in an Iranian or Middle Eastern shop, make sure you grab them. In this dish you get the wonderful combination of slow-cooked meat, plus a fresh mint and almond crunch.

Chop the onion and celery into small cubes or mirepoix. In a heavy frying pan over a medium heat, fry the mirepoix in 1 tbsp of the olive oil and 1 tbsp of the butter until golden, stirring frequently. Add the fresh almonds, chopped herbs and sugar and sauté for a further 10 minutes. Stir in the tomato purée and let it 'cook out' for a couple of minutes so that the raw smell evaporates. Then add the stock or water, dried mint, lemon or lime juice, salt and pepper.

Heat the remaining oil and butter in another frying pan and brown the chicken pieces with the turmeric until golden. Make sure to just sear the chicken – don't overcook it, as it will cook further with the almond mixture.

Now add the chicken to the almond mixture, cover and simmer for another 30–40 minutes or so until the meat is fork-tender and all the flavours come together. Add the saffron liquid 10 minutes before the end of the cooking time. Check the seasoning: you may need to add more sugar or extra lemon or lime juice to balance the dish out.

Serve with *kateh* (soft cooked rice, page 109) or Polo Ba Taadig (perfect fluffy rice, page 106).

TORSHIYEH PESTEH
PICKLED PISTACHIOS

ترشی پسته

fresh pistachios
or plain unroasted pistachios, shells removed

white vinegar
or white wine vinegar or white grape vinegar

Did you know that the word pistachio comes from the Persian *pesteh*? Pistachios have been cultivated in Iran for thousands of years, and are used in savoury dishes as well as desserts. I think they are best enjoyed plain as a snack, either roasted or fresh, when in season, and dipped in rock salt. This recipe ideally uses fresh pistachios, which are only on sale once a year. You can make it with dried pistachios, but soak them first (see below).

Fresh pistachios have a thick pink leathery skin that must be peeled off before cracking the immature soft shell. Inside the fresh nut is bright green, tender as a young pea and delicious. The bigger the pistachios, the more highly prized they are, and the colour must be deep green. (Smaller paler ones are mostly ground up to use in cooking.) Here is a delightful *torshi* or pickle recipe.

If using dried pistachios, put them in a bowl, cover with cold water and leave in the fridge for about 2 days. Drain the soaked pistachios and remove the thin outer skin. It should come off easily.

If using fresh pistachios, remove the leathery outer layer and the shells but leave intact the thin skins that protect the nut.

Sterilise a selection of jars and lids. Add the pistachios and fill the jars with vinegar. Seal and leave in a cool dark place for at least 10 weeks before serving.

آجیل

AJEEL
PERSIAN TRAIL MIX

Ajeel is a mix of nuts and dried fruits and is a staple snack in Iran. There are endless variations – each family has its own recipe, and in every home there's almost always a bowl of *ajeel* on the table in case of unexpected visitors.

Ajeel is served on the longest night of the year, Shabeh Yalda or winter solstice. Yalda, which usually falls on 20 or 21 December, is one of the key Zoroastrian festivals, although it in fact has its roots even further back in Mithraism, celebrating the solstice as the birth of the sun-god.

In the olden days there was a version of *ajeel* called Nokhodchi Keshmesh (raisins and roasted chickpeas) for children's lunch boxes – my grandmother often added a few muskwillow seed *noghls* (sugared nuts, page 78) to it.

The mixtures below follow traditional recipes, which specify no seeds in sweet *ajeel* and no walnuts in salty *ajeel*. But you can vary the ingredients and create your own.

AJEELI-E-SHOOR
SALTY TRAIL MIX
(NB use salted nuts)

roasted pistachios

roasted almonds

roasted cashews (a relatively new addition)

pumpkin seeds

watermelon seeds

salted roasted chickpeas

AJEEL-E-SHIRIN
SWEET TRAIL MIX
(NB use unsalted nuts)

raisins

roasted pistachios

roasted almonds

walnuts

roasted hazelnuts

cashew nuts (a relatively new addition)

roasted chickpeas

white mulberries

miniature white figs

apricots

Buslogh (a kind of Turkish delight stuffed with walnuts and cut into rings)

Joz Hendi (dried fruit roll stuffed with icing sugar and spices and shaped into balls)

هالق / هاروست

HAROSET
PERSIAN-JEWISH SWEET WITH NUTS
AND DRIED FRUIT

2kg (4lb) 17 cups shelled
pistachios

1.5kg (3lb) 12 cups shelled
walnuts

1.5kg (3lb) 8 cups shelled
hazelnuts

1.5kg (3lb) 10 cups sultanas

1kg (2lb) 6 cups almonds

1kg (2lb) 6 cups cashews

1kg (2lb) 6 cups dates

2kg (4lb) apples,
peeled and cored

2 bottles sweet
pomegranate juice
(or unsweetened with 3–4 tbsp
sugar added, to taste)

1 bottle sweet kosher wine
or any sweet wine

2 tbsp readymade *halegh*
spices or *advieh* (Persian spice
mix, see page 204)

This fruit and nut mix is a Persian-Jewish recipe, a variation of the traditional Jewish fruit and nut paste that represents the bricks and mortar made by the Israelites as slaves in ancient Egypt. It's also known as Halegh.

Jews have been recorded as living in Iran since 721BC and the country still boasts the largest Jewish community in the Middle East outside Israel. In the mid-19th century there were Jewish schools in Tehran and a weekly newspaper called *Shalom*. By the time the Reza Shah came to power in 1925, Jews were fairly integrated into the community. However, his alignment with Nazi Germany could have led them to suffer the same fate as European Jews, had he not been forced to abdicate.

This recipe was given to me by Dora Levy Mossanen's mother Parvin. Dora, an Iranian Jew, fled to the US after the Islamic revolution. She is the author of *Harem* and *Courtesan*, novels set in ancient Persia. The recipe feeds 40 guests – Jewish Iranians are fond of entertaining!

Place all the ingredients in a blender and process to your preferred consistency. Some people like creamy *halegh*, others slightly crunchy – you can adjust the texture by varying the amount of wine and juice you add. Similarly you can adjust the spices to taste. Finally, roll the blended *halegh* into a log shape using your hands.

ADASS POLO BA KOOFTEH GHELGHELI

MEATBALLS WITH LENTILLED RICE,
STICKY DATES AND RAISINS

For the adassi rice:

800g (1lb 10oz) 4 cups rice

300g (10oz) 1½ cups brown lentils, soaked for 2-3 hours

50-75g (2-3oz) ¼- ⅓ cup melted butter, ghee or safflower oil, plus 1 tbsp extra for topping

1½ tbsp natural yogurt

⅓ tsp saffron threads, pounded

1 tsp cinnamon

For the meatballs:

1 small onion, grated

1 tsp sea salt

few twists of pepper

½ tsp turmeric

500g (1lb) lean ground beef or lamb

oil, for frying

For the raisin and date mixture:

1 large onion, grated and liquid drained off

1 tbsp butter (or use more oil)

½ tbsp oil

½ tsp cinnamon

twist of black pepper

10-12 pitted dates

50g (2oz) ½ cup raisins

This is one of those heavenly dishes that people can't get enough of. I'd say it is a very Middle Eastern dish, packed with lamb, lentils, cinnamon-infused rice and sweet raisins and dates tossed in butter. It is lovely served with yogurt and herbs. The best dates come from the city of Bam, known for its beautiful citadel, which was mostly destroyed in an earthquake on Boxing Day 2003. Bam dates are juicy and wet as opposed to chewy Madjool ones. Think fudge versus caramel. If you have to use ordinary dates, plump them up in water first for 10–15 minutes or steam them on top of the rice as it cooks. For a vegetarian version simply leave out the meatballs.

Prepare the rice according to the method for Polo Ba Taadig (perfect fluffy rice, page 106), up to draining and cooling. Set aside, reserving two ladlefuls. Place the lentils in a pan, add water to just cover and simmer for 15–30 minutes maximum, until they are soft but not falling apart. Drain and mix with the rice, making sure not to crush them.

Heat the melted butter, ghee or oil in a heavy-based saucepan with 75ml (3fl oz) ⅓ cup water, the yogurt, saffron and reserved rice and mix well. Spread the mixture over the base of the pan, then start layering the rice and lentil mixture, sprinkling it with cinnamon as you go. Shape the mixture into a pyramid at the top. Finish cooking the pyramid of rice following the Polo Ba Taadig method.

While the rice is cooking, make the meatballs. Knead the grated onion, salt, pepper and turmeric into the meat for about 5 minutes until paste-like. Form into small hazelnut-sized balls. Heat the oil in a shallow pan and fry the meatballs on a medium-high heat on one side for about 2 minutes or until golden. Turn them over and fry the other side for another 2–3 minutes. Remove and place on a plate.

Meanwhile, prepare the raisin and date mixture. Sauté the onion with the butter and oil until dark gold, add the cinnamon and pepper and then the dates, stirring constantly. Add the raisins last as they can burn very easily. Stir just until they begin to puff up and are warm.

To serve, layer the rice with the meatballs, then top the whole dish with the caramelised raisins and dates. Serve with cool yogurt.

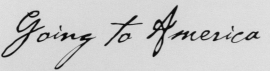

Going to America

My father's family comes from Tabriz, in the Iranian Province of Azarbaijan (not to be confused with the nearby country of Azerbaijan), near the Turkish border. The region is known for its history as well as for its rolling green hills, high mountains and beautiful clear blue lakes. Some people claim that the cuisine of this region is the most lip-smackingly delicious and more-ish in all of Iran.

Women here cook heartily, kneading giant Tabrizi meatballs (which sometimes contain a whole poussin!), stirring their *ash* (soups) for hours, patting *cotelettes* (meat and potato patties, page 160) and frying them to perfection, and stuffing and rolling *dolmehs* (stuffed vine leaves, page 46) by the hundred. These women are called *Shir-Zan* (lionesses) because they manage their homes to a T and are always ready with fresh fruits, homemade sweets and meals whenever anyone calls. The people of the region are often known as Azeris or colloquially as Torks – someone of Turkish descent, the second biggest ethnic group in Iran after Persians.

My paternal great-grandfather, Shir Mohammad Khan e Saadlou, and his wife, Zivar Khanoum, were also landowners, like my mother's side of the family. Shir Mohammad was a nobleman and ruled a khanate or large clan, during Imperial Persia. To his father's dismay, my grandfather Ebrahim broke away from family tradition: he became a government official.

My father, Manouchehr Saadlou, nicknamed Michel, had other plans for his life, too. He wanted to leave for America. To the disapproval of his conservative (though not religious) family, in the 1960s he made his way overland to Europe, with not much in his pocket, and from there sailed to America. He learned English and washed dishes by night to support himself through engineering school. Similar stories abound among Iranian immigrants, especially after the revolution.

He later became the manager of an exclusive club within the Beverly Hilton, frequented by the stars of the silver screen. It was and still is the home of the annual Golden Globe Awards and is where Richard Nixon gave his last press conference.

Michel developed his skills and headed back home, running a famous casino in Tehran, before going on to open Iran's first and most exclusive French fine-dining restaurant, *Chez Michel*. Back then, being a restaurateur in Iran wasn't considered much of a job as it was in the West, but he decided to follow his passion.

At *Chez Michel* the walls were panelled with cherry oak and the silverware and trolleys came from France. He flew in a chef and maître d' from Paris and ended up creating a venue for power lunches, where the Shah used to dine with his family.

My father was a fantastically handsome man, over six feet tall, always impeccably dressed, and he knew how to put on the charm. He was also an extremely skilled businessman and a great visionary. He socialised with royals and celebrities of Iran with the ease and confidence that came from working hard and being self-made.

FAMILY
MEMOIR

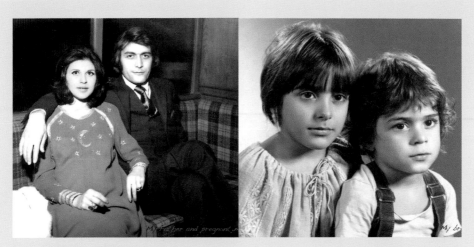

My mother and father   **Me and my brother**

That a French restaurant would prove such a hit in Iran is not so surprising. Persian stews are almost identical to their French counterparts. Except for the bouquet garni (which Iranians replace with *advieh*), they both fry onions along with the meat to sear it, then add stock and let the dish simmer slowly until the meat is so tender it falls apart. It is said that in pre-Islamic Iran, stews were made with wine rather than water or stock, similar to *coq au vin*. And the seasoning in Persian cooking is also mild. Like the French, Iranians prefer to showcase the freshness of their ingredients rather than mask it.

Once the revolution hit hard, my father lost everything, as did many other people. He went back to America and opened a French-Californian restaurant in Beverly Hills by the name of Club 22. It quickly became a place where celebrities came to dine and Hollywood magnates did business deals.

I will never forget my father's usual 'airport pick up' speech whenever we flew in from London in the mid-1980s: 'God bless America, land of the free. You can do anything you want here. This is where dreams come true, if you work enough for them!' He would take my brother and me out and give us fusion foods – fish tacos, hamburgers on baguettes with avocados – things we weren't quite sure we liked. We would roll our eyes at each other. But we later realised how much he taught us.

Even when we were much younger, my dad would make us flambéed crêpes, flipping them just right. Our first books were not children's story books, but the cookbooks my father collected. We would pore over them for hours and hours, looking at pages of cassoulets, duck à l'orange, intricate desserts and names for cuts of meat. So different from Persian cuisine, yet somehow not that alien. It was then that I found my passion, around the age of five, and started experimenting with frying onions and making jelly...

FAMILY
MEMOIR

نان نخودچی

NOON NOKHODCHI

CHICKPEA SHORTBREADS WITH CARDAMOM

These delicate cookies are distinctly Persian – dense and buttery, like a very crumbly, slightly moist shortbread. Noon Nokhodchi are usually bought readymade. But women are also starting to run small businesses from home, producing them in simple shapes. This is my Khaleh Eshrat's recipe. Roasted chickpea flour is sold in Middle Eastern food shops. If you can't get hold of any, buy ordinary chickpea flour – often labelled gram flour – from the supermarket and roast it yourself. Put the flour on a tray and bake in a preheated oven at 180°C/350°F/ Gas Mark 4 for about 12-15 minutes until golden, stirring once during baking. Let it cool before using.

1 very small organic egg (or add 1 tbsp of water instead)

250g (8oz) 2 cups icing sugar

125ml (4fl oz) ½ cup safflower oil or any tasteless oil, gently warmed

125g (4oz) ½ cup butter or ghee, melted and kept warm (or use an extra 125ml/4fl oz oil instead)

500g (1lb) 3 cups roasted chickpea flour, sifted (see above)

¼ tsp ground cardamom

3 tbsp pistachio slivers, to decorate

Beat the egg in a glass if using – you only need half for the recipe. The next step can either be done by hand or with a food processor fitted with a paddle. Place the sugar, egg (if using) or water and the warm oil and butter (or warm oil) in the bowl and mix for about 2–3 minutes until pale and creamy. Or beat for 5 minutes by hand. Add the chickpea flour and cardamom, and mix for a further 3 minutes in the machine or 5–7 minutes by hand. Don't be tempted to add any liquid, the ingredients will eventually come together in a dough.

Place the dough on a floured board and knead for another minute or so until it is no longer sticky. Line a tray with parchment paper. Push and flatten the dough on to the tray so that it is about 2.5cm (1in) thick. Place in the fridge for at least an hour to harden.

Meanwhile, preheat the oven to 150°C/300°F/Gas Mark 2. Prepare a non-stick baking tray or line one with a Silpat non-stick baking mat. Take out the dough and use cookie cutters to stamp out clover leaves, flowers or even simple circles the size of a macadamia nut. Place the cookies on the tray. They won't rise or spread that much so leave only 2.5cm (1in) or so between them. Bake for about 25–30 minutes. Meanwhile, halve the pistachio slivers with a knife.

Don't allow the cookies to colour; check the bases and if they're golden and slightly pinkish, then they're done. Take them out of the oven and push one pistachio sliver in the middle of each cookie. Leave to cool completely before removing them from the tray or they will crumble. They last about a month in a container in the fridge or three months in the freezer.

SHAMI
CHICKPEA PATTIES
OR MINI SAVOURY
DOUGHNUTS

Shamis take me back to my grandmother's time. She said that the best ones have a *pook* (hollow) feel to them, meaning they should be light and airy. (In fact *shami pook* is another name for them.) Iranian *shamis* are made with chickpea flour and a little bicarbonate of soda, which makes it easy to achieve a light dough. My auntie Mahin Zarinpanjeh, who is a renowned cook, composer and pianist, gave me this recipe. Use ground meat – the easier option – or cook a piece of lean meat then either pound it or pass it through an old-fashioned mincer.

Put the lamb on the bone in a large saucepan, cover with water so that there is 5–8cm (2–3in) depth of water above the meat, and bring to the boil. Boil for a few minutes, skim then add the oil, chopped onions, turmeric, salt and pepper. Reduce the heat to its lowest setting, cover and cook for about 2½ hours, adding the cinnamon about 30 minutes before the end of the cooking time. Check occasionally and add more water if necessary. The meat will be falling off the bone and there will be very little liquid left in the pot.

Discard the bone and put the meat and onion in a food processor, along with the eggs, chickpea flour, bicarbonate of soda, salt and the saffron liquid if using. Taste the mixture: add more salt if necessary.

If making the *shamis* with ground lamb, start the recipe at this point and put the meat, oil, onions, turmeric, salt, pepper and cinnamon in the food processor, along with all the other ingredients, except the oil for frying. Whizz until you get a smooth paste. Or use an old-fashioned mincer if you have one, for a more authentic result. Do it twice to get a smooth paste.

Have a bowl of warm water to dip your hands in and start making the *shamis*. Take a spoonful of the paste and roll into a ball the size of a walnut then flatten it on a chopping board. Pick it up and poke a hole in it with your little finger to make it look like a doughnut. Prepare all the *shamis* before frying them in enough hot oil to cover, over a medium-high heat.

Fry *shamis* made from the simmered lamb for about 2 minutes on each side or until they're dark golden, and the outside nice and crisp.

Fry *shamis* made with raw meat for 3–4 minutes on each side to cook through. Lay them on a plate lined with paper towels to remove excess oil. Serve hot or cold with Sabzi Khordan (fresh herbs, page 132) and *torshi* (pickles, page 84).

500g (1lb) piece of lamb on the bone but with fat removed (or 500g/1lb ground lamb)

2 tbsp oil

2 large onions, chopped

½ tsp turmeric

salt and pepper

½ tsp cinnamon

2 eggs

400g (13oz) 2½ cups roasted chickpea flour (see opposite)

½ tsp bicarbonate of soda

1½ tsp salt, plus extra to taste

¼ tsp saffron threads, pounded then dissolved in 1–2 tbsp hot water (optional)

safflower oil or any oil, for frying

ADASSI
SLOW-COOKED LENTIL SOUP
SPRINKLED WITH
HOGWEED POWDER

400g (13oz) 2 cups brown lentils or Puy lentils, soaked overnight in 1 litre (1¾ pints) 4 cups water

1 medium onion, chopped into small cubes or 10 pearl onions, peeled and left whole

2 tbsp olive oil

½ tsp turmeric

1 large potato, cut into 5cm (2in) cubes

salt and pepper

1 tbsp butter (optional)

fresh lemon juice, yogurt and *golpar* (hogweed powder), to serve

My mum makes the best lentil soup. Something between a French lentil *cassoulet* and an Indian *dhal*, this is a delicious warming dish. Street vendors sell Adassi in the cold winter months: you eat it sprinkled with *golpar* or Persian hogweed powder.

Golpar is a native wild plant from the humid mountains of northern Iran. Its seeds are ground and used as a spice, and thanks to its medicinal benefits – it alleviates wind – it is often used in dishes with beans and lentils. It's also sprinkled on pomegranate seeds, on hot cooked potatoes and added to pickles. *Golpar* is sold in Middle Eastern stores, sometimes mislabelled as angelica.

Drain all the water from the lentils. Tip them in a saucepan, add 900ml (1½ pints) 3½ cups fresh water, bring to the boil and boil on a high heat for a few minutes. Skim, lower the heat, cover halfway with a lid and simmer for about an hour.

Meanwhile, fry the onion in the olive oil until light gold and translucent (not dark). Add the turmeric and fry for a few minutes. Add the mixture to the lentils along with the cubed potato. Add another 125ml (4fl oz) ½ cup of water if the soup looks as if it needs it. Add the salt and pepper and cook for another 45–60 minutes or until the lentils and potatoes are cooked. The potatoes will have melted a little into the soup, which is exactly what you are looking for. Remove from the heat, add the butter if using and serve with either fresh lemon juice, cool creamy natural yogurt or a sprinkle of *golpar*.

NOGHL
DAINTY WHITE SUGARED ALMONDS

500g (1lb) 2 cups caster sugar

125ml (4fl oz) ½ cup rose water

175g (6oz) 1 cup unsalted slivered almonds, blanched

Whole or slivered almonds are simply coated in sugar and transformed into elegant frosted white sweets scented with rose water. *Noghl* are served at weddings and given away as favours in tuile bags, to symbolise a sweet marriage. In fact they remind me of little brides in their white wedding dresses. The nuts are also handed round at *Norooz* (Persian New Year) celebrations, and served instead of sugar lumps along with hot tea. My grandmother had them mixed in with her sugar lumps in the sugar bowl. *Noghl* also used to be added to *ajeel* (Persian trail mix, page 68) to sweeten it for children.

Place the sugar in a pan with 250ml (8fl oz) 1 cup water, bring to the boil and boil for about 20 minutes. Add the rose water, bring back to the boil and cook for another 2 minutes on a low heat or until a sugar thermometer shows 130°C/266°F.

Place the almond slivers in another saucepan with a firm handle and slowly add the sugar syrup to the almonds while shaking them. They will magically turn white and frosted-looking. Do this slowly otherwise the almonds will not be evenly coated.

Another way I've experimented with is to place the almonds in a food processor fitted with a paddle and slowly pour in the hot syrup while the machine is running. Use a low speed so as not to break the nuts. Place the frosted nuts on a baking sheet lined with parchment paper or a Silpat non-stick baking mat, and leave to cool before separating them.

Whole almonds and slivered almonds with a fragrant frosting of sugar and rose water. Also on the table are *gaz* – Iranian nougat – and a dish of *nabat* (rock sugar crystals, *top right*)

GONDI
JEWISH-IRANIAN SOUP WITH CHICKEN
AND ROASTED CHICKPEA DUMPLINGS

This recipe may sound surprising given the current relationship between Iran and Israel. But Jews have been a part of Persian history for 2,500 years. Iranian Jews eat the same food as everyone else in Iran. Maybe that's why they consider themselves to be Iranians first, then Jews. A few years ago, I was invited to Saturday morning prayers by Rabbi Hakhan Yousseff Hamadani Cohen. This is his recipe. Gondi soup is one of the dishes that Persian Jews call their own. I've modified his version slightly as his dumplings were the size of tennis balls! He says you don't have to make them quite so big...

Place the chicken in a large pot and cover with cold water. Bring to the boil and boil on high for a few minutes. Skim then add the bay leaf, onion, garlic, celery, carrot and turmeric. Cover and simmer on a low heat for about 1½ hours, skimming occasionally. Add the pounded saffron 10 minutes before the end of the cooking time.

Discard the celery stalk and bay leaf, and remove the whole chicken or chicken pieces – set them aside for a Salad Olivier (chicken salad, page 156) or another dish.

Make the dumplings while the soup cooks. Put all the ingredients in a large bowl and knead by hand for a good 10 minutes or put them in a food processor and whizz rapidly without overmixing. Have a small bowl of warm water to dip your hands in and start shaping the dumplings. For a more elegant dish, go for golf-ball size.

Bring the soup to a simmer before adding the dumplings. Add the Omani limes at the same time if using. Cook for 30 minutes. Serve with bread and Sabzi Khordan (fresh herbs, page 132) and *torshi* (pickles, page 84). You can also serve Gondi like Ab Gousht (lamb shank soup, page 60), lifting out the dumplings to eat with bread and handing the soup round separately.

For the soup:

1 whole chicken or equivalent chicken pieces, with skin left on

1 bay leaf

1 medium onion, thinly sliced

2 garlic cloves, skinned and roughly chopped

1 celery stalk with leaves

1 medium carrot, cut into 7.5cm (3in) pieces

1 tsp turmeric

½ tsp saffron threads, pounded

salt and pepper, to taste

3-4 dried Omani limes, pierced with the tip of a knife (optional – you can leave these out as they tend to darken the soup)

For the dumplings:

500g (1lb) ground chicken – a mixture of breast and thigh is best

1 large onion, grated and liquid drained off

100g (3½oz) 1 cup roasted chickpea flour (see page 74)

1 egg

½ tsp turmeric

2 tbsp finely chopped coriander or parsley

1 tbsp finely chopped tarragon

2 tsp salt

few twists of pepper

سبزیجات

CHAPTER THREE

VEGETABLES

TORSHIYEH PIYAZ
CRUNCHY PICKLED PEARL ONIONS

1kg (2lb) pearl or button
onions, peeled

1 tbsp salt

1½ litres (2½ pints) 6 cups
white wine vinegar

bunch of fresh tarragon

Onions are a staple in Iranian cuisine. They're sweated
for stews, chopped and kneaded in meatballs, put in
stuffings, deep fried to scatter over appetisers and hearty
soups, and added to marinades to tenderise *kababs*. They
are also used, along with turmeric, to cut out or mask
the smell of meat. Iranians don't like the natural smell of
cooked meat: they find it harsh and unrefined.

Usually white or yellow onions are used – red onions
less so. If raw onions are called for in a recipe, they are
sometimes soaked in water overnight to remove the
harshness and lessen their bite. Iranians are very careful
about smelling of onions or garlic and watch what they
eat on important occasions, whether it's a business
meeting, a date or meeting the prospective in-laws.
Thankfully this pickled onion recipe is not so strong as to
alienate people and it's oh-so-simple to make.

Cut an x at the bottom of the onions so that the vinegar can
penetrate them. Whisk the salt and vinegar in a stainless steel pan
over gentle heat so that they blend. Leave to cool completely. Place
the onions in sterilised jars along with the sprigs of tarragon and pour
over the cooled vinegar mixture, making sure it covers the onions.
Seal and store for 2–3 months before using.

Seer Torshi (pickled garlic, page 86), Torshiyeh Piyaz (pickled
pearl onions, this page), Khiar Shoor (pickled cucumbers,
page 188) and Torshiyeh Liteh (pickled aubergines, page 187)

SEER TORSHI
AGED PICKLED GARLIC

500g (1lb) garlic bulbs, nice fresh ones

1.2 litres (2 pints) 5 cups white wine vinegar, white grape vinegar or white vinegar

Pickled garlic is like wine: the longer ago it was bottled, the better it is! We have some at home that is 20 years old. The bulbs are black, soft and sweet, and taste a little like aged balsamic vinegar. But Seer Torshi is best eaten when it is around six to seven years old. You can buy it from Middle Eastern shops but it will be young and crunchy.

Pickled garlic comes from the north, in the Caspian region of Iran, where they eat lots of garlic as it goes very well with the climate and the 'cold' fish dishes of the region (see *Unani*, page 16). I cannot tell you how delicious this *torshi* is when eaten with Mirza Ghassemi (garlicky smoky aubergines, page 89) or Baghali Ghatogh (fresh broad beans with dill, page 184) and *kateh* (soft cooked rice, page 109) while sitting in front of the Caspian sea and feeling the breeze on your skin.

Make sure the garlic bulbs are clean and dry. Peel off one layer of skin. Put the bulbs in sterilised jars and cover with vinegar. Seal and store in a cool dark place for at least 2 months before eating.

MORABAYEH BADEMJOON
AUBERGINE CONSERVE SCENTED WITH ROSE WATER

1kg (2lb) baby seedless aubergines, kept whole

500g (1lb) 2 cups preserving sugar

75ml (3fl oz) ⅓ cup rose water

5 cardamom pods, whole but lightly crushed

1 tbsp lemon or lime juice

Iranians love aubergines: they put them in stews, stuff them with a mixture of rice and meat, purée them for dips and also pickle them or turn them into sweet jams as here. Iranians always cook aubergines well – never *al dente* as you might find them in Thai cooking, for example. Buy small aubergines in Middle Eastern or Thai shops. This conserve is usually served with hot fragrant tea.

Blanch the baby aubergines in boiling water for about 5 minutes then drain. Boil the sugar and 1½ litres (2½ pints) 6 cups water in a preserving pan for about 1 minute, then add the aubergines one by one. Once you've added them all to the pan, let them cook in the syrup for about 20 minutes or until the syrup is nice and thick.

Add the rose water, cardamom pods and lemon or lime juice and let the mixture come back to the boil again and bubble away for 2–3 minutes. Pot in sterilised jars.

MIRZA GHASSEMI
GARLICKY SMOKY AUBERGINES
WITH TOMATOES AND EGGS

2 large garlic bulbs, cut in half

50ml (2fl oz) ¼ cup olive oil, plus extra for brushing

4-5 medium aubergines, left whole, skin on

1 tsp turmeric

¾ tsp salt

few twists of pepper

1 tbsp tomato purée

4 medium tomatoes, skinned and diced

3 large eggs, lightly whisked or kept whole

100g (3½oz) butter

1 garlic clove, grated, to serve

Mirza Ghassemi is a recipe from the Caspian region of Mazandaran. It's full of zesty garlic, smoky charred aubergines and juicy fresh tomatoes. Mixed with turmeric and eggs, it has a lovely golden red colour and makes a fantastic dip or a very light lunch served with *lavash* bread or even with *kateh* (soft cooked rice, page 109). Some people prefer to scramble the eggs into the dish, while others crack the eggs straight into the mixture and let them cook to perfection sunny side up. Fresh turmeric used to be grated into the dish but now it is the norm to use powdered. My Auntie Maryam adds butter to it and even though it isn't traditional, it makes it extra yummy.

Brush the garlic bulbs with some olive oil. Prick the aubergines with a knife or fork. Grill the aubergines and garlic for 20–30 minutes. The skins will be charred.

Peel away and discard the aubergine and garlic skins. Mash the flesh together (or chop it), until you get a chunky consistency.

Heat the olive oil in a saucepan and add the turmeric, salt, pepper and aubergine mixture. Sauté over a medium heat. After about 7–8 minutes, add the tomato purée and the diced tomatoes and cook gently, uncovered, for 20 minutes or until no liquid is left.

Then you have a choice. Either add the whisked eggs and the butter into the mixture and stir until cooked through, or dot the mixture with the butter and break the eggs on top of the mixture and leave to cook. Or fry them in the butter and serve on the side. Grate a fresh garlic clove over the dish and it's ready to eat. Serve with rice, bread, Sabzi Khordan (fresh herbs, page 132) and cool yogurt.

My Mamani

My maternal grandmother Talat was a rare gem. Beautiful, smart, with a perfect little round head. She lit up a room like a jewel or a piece of gold, as if a light was reflected on her face. In fact she was nicknamed Tala, meaning gold in Persian. In her youth, she had fair hair, green eyes and pale honey-coloured skin. But when I knew her she had straight white candyfloss hair, pink cheeks, delicately lined eyebrows. She wore glasses and always dressed immaculately with a patent leather handbag and shoes, and her trademark pearl earrings or necklace.

At the tender age of seven, she lost her mother Tooran-Taj Lesan ol Salteneh Ghahremani in tragic and mysterious circumstances. Her father Salar Mansoureh Ghafar Yeganeh remarried three times and had many more children, who formed strong relationships with my grandmother. But as Talat was her father's favourite child, he married her off to his best friend Mr Borhan when she was only 15. He was the information minister, a very high position at the time, and their lives were a series of functions, events and parties for politicians and foreign dignitaries. She told me how a British diplomat wrote to her, thanking her for his stay and remarking how lovely my grandmother's cousin was, but 'what a shame about the moustache!' Back then some women drew a dark line just above their lips as makeup.

Although my grandmother had nothing but good to say about her husband, he unfortunately could not give her children. So when, at a party, she locked eyes with my grandfather (whose own wife was unable to have children), no one could stop them falling in love. Her sister Effat also fell in love with my grandfather's brother Hashem. So two brothers married two sisters and bore many children.

Tala was loved by so many people. There was something about her that made people feel good about themselves. They just wanted to sit by her and were willing to do anything for her. Maybe it was her beauty or maybe it was something to do with what she always told us: 'Nothing is more important than a good character.'

Mamani is an Iranian term for grandmother that also means adorable or endearing. My *Mamani* was also an amazing chef – not a cook. She rarely went in the kitchen when she was younger – she had cooks to do that. But when she became a grandmother, she showed us that she was a master at creating dishes and pairing ingredients. Her soups were famous. She would throw in whatever she had to hand but she also thought things through – the textures, taste, amounts, combinations.

One of the first things I ever cooked was fried onions in *Mamani*'s kitchen. She would put a stool for me to stand on and tie a yellow apron with lace and sunflowers on it round my waist and let me stir the onions. She patiently explained things to me and made me feel that I couldn't do any wrong. She made me see food as something magical and delightful.

FAMILY
MEMOIR

My grandmother aged 15 (*left*) with her cousin

FAMILY
MEMOIR

KHORESHTEH ESFENAJ

SPINACH STEW WITH DRIED PLUMS OR PRUNES

1 large white onion, finely sliced

3 tbsp oil or olive oil

1 tbsp butter (optional)

500g (1lb) de-boned lamb or stewing beef, cut into 4–5cm (1½–2in) cubes, or 1kg (2lb) chicken breasts on the bone

2 garlic cloves, finely chopped

½ tsp turmeric

500ml (17fl oz) 2 cups hot unsalted chicken stock or water

5–6 spring onions, finely chopped

625g (1¼lb) about 25 cups chopped fresh spinach, or 150g (5oz) 1 cup frozen

1½ tsp salt

juice of 1 small lime or medium lemon

juice of 1 tangerine or small orange

1 tsp brown sugar (optional)

few twists of pepper

10–12 Persian dried yellow plums (*aloo zard*) or small black prunes

Spinach is indigenous to Iran; its name comes from the Persian word *esfenaj*. The delicious combination of spinach and prunes – things we all hated to eat as children – comes together beautifully in this dish. The deep green earthy taste of spinach coupled with the sweet and sour dried yellow plums (*aloo zard*) or prunes and the tender lamb is exquisite. Please make sure not to overcook the spinach so it stays green and fresh. Orange juice helps bind it all together and gives it a lovely aroma and flavour. This recipe is equally delicious without meat.

Sauté the onion over a medium-high heat in 1 tbsp oil, and the butter if using, until golden. Add the meat, garlic and turmeric and stir until the meat is seared. Add the hot stock or water and simmer slowly for about 1 hour. If you're making the dish with chicken, reduce the cooking time to 50 minutes.

Meanwhile, sauté the spring onions with the remaining 2 tbsp oil until golden and caramelised but not burnt. This will add depth to the stew. Add the chopped spinach and stir over a high heat until the leaves are wilted and there is no liquid left in the pan. If using frozen spinach, defrost and squeeze out any water beforehand.

Add this to the meat mixture along with the salt, citrus juices, half of the sugar, and the pepper. Cook for another 20 minutes or so. If using *aloo zard* you will need to boil them first for about 10 minutes to soften them, then drain. Add the plums or prunes 15 minutes before the end of cooking time. Check that the meat is cooked and taste to see if you need to add the rest of the sugar. Serve with rice (*polo*, page 106 or *kateh*, page 109).

TIP: You can substitute 1 tbsp of green *advieh* (page 204) for the individual spices. Don't try using Agen prunes instead of Persian dried plums – they are too sweet. And if you can buy only large prunes, reduce the quantity.

BOORANIYEH ESFENAJ
SPINACH AND YOGURT DIP

1 very small or half
a white onion, diced

1–2 tbsp oil

2 garlic cloves, diced very
finely

625g (1¼lb) about 25 cups
chopped fresh spinach, or
150g (5oz) 1 cup frozen

500g (1lb) 2 cups strained
Greek yogurt, or natural yogurt

1 rounded tsp salt

twist of black pepper

warm bread, to serve

This dish dates back to the 11th century and was written about in the poetry of Naser-e Kosrow. Named in honour of Poorandokht, a Sassanian queen, *booranis* are usually made with yogurt mixed with a single cooked vegetable, be it spinach, beets, courgette or aubergine. (The cucumber version is Mast o Khiar or cold cucumber soup, page 136.) This recipe was such a favourite of my grandmother's that she named one of her dogs Boorani!

Sauté the onion in the oil. Add the garlic at the last minute before it all turns translucent. Set aside.

Cook the spinach in a steamer for a couple of minutes until limp but still green. Or place the spinach in a pan, cover with a lid and let it 'wilt' on a medium heat. It won't need any water since spinach naturally has enough juice in its leaves (unless you overcook it, in which case it'll stick to the pan). Quick cooking ensures that all the vitamins stay in the spinach and it keeps its green colour. If using frozen spinach, defrost and squeeze out any liquid beforehand, then sauté. Or sauté it from frozen, but let the liquid evaporate before using.

Let the spinach cool. Chop it further and stir it into the yogurt. Place in a serving dish and add the sautéed onion and garlic (although you can omit this altogether if you prefer), and sprinkle with salt and pepper. Eat with some lovely hot bread for dipping.

ASHE MASH KHALEH ESHRAT

HEARTY MUNG BEAN
SOUP WITH
CARAMELISED
PEARL ONIONS

500g (1lb) 2½ cups dried
mung beans, soaked overnight

1½ litres (2½ pints) 6 cups
hot unsalted chicken stock
or vegetable stock or water

50g (2oz) ⅓ cup rice,
soaked for an hour or so in a bowl
of water, then drained

20–25 pearl or button
onions or 12–15 small shallots,
kept whole

1 tbsp turmeric

¾–1 tsp salt

few twists of pepper

For the topping:

1 medium onion, finely sliced

2 tbsp safflower oil or
flavourless oil

This was my aunt's, Khaleh Eshrat's, favourite soup.
Whenever we went to Ghazvin to pay respects at
maghbareyeh famil (my family's tomb), we would visit
Khaleh and she would set out a feast for us. This dish,
along with Asheh Jo (barley potage, page 126), is a hearty
winter soup and a nutritious vegetarian dish. Some
people add herbs and spinach but my Khaleh's version is
simple, so that you can really taste the mung beans.

After eating it we sat at the *korsee* (a table covered with
a thick blanket and with an electric heater underneath)
with cushions all around. We would tuck ourselves under
the blanket and take a short sweet nap, and have fragrant
tea and homemade *baghlava* (page 202) when we awoke.

In a large saucepan, boil the mung beans with 1 litre (1¾ pints)
4 cups of the stock or water. The level of the liquid needs to be twice
the depth of the beans, so add more if you need to. Bring the beans
to a fierce boil. After about 10 minutes add 250ml (8fl oz) 1 cup cold
water and watch as the bean skins float to the surface. When all
the skins have come off, skim them off and discard, but reserve a
tablespoon or two to put back in the soup later when you mash or
blend it a little. Khaleh did this so that her soup had more texture, but
you don't have to do it if you don't want to. After skimming off the
skins, add the rice, lower the heat and cook for about 30–40 minutes,
skimming once in a while if any froth appears.

Add the onions or shallots, turmeric and the salt and pepper and
cook for another 45 minutes or until the onions are tender. At this
stage you need to stir the soup frequently otherwise it will catch at the
bottom of the pan. Mash it a bit with the spoon as you go along. Add
up to another 500ml (17fl oz) 2 cups of stock or water if the soup is
getting too thick. If necessary, remove some of the soup and blend
with a hand-held blender or lift out some of the beans and push them
through a sieve back into the pan – you're aiming for a soup with
some texture, rather than a smooth soup.

Meanwhile, fry the onion for the topping in the oil until crispy and
golden. Pour the soup into a tureen and top with caramelised onions.

مرغ ترش

MORGHEH TORSH
SOUR CHICKEN STEW
WITH SPLIT PEAS AND HERBS

2 tbsp yellow split peas

1 small onion, cut into cubes

2 tbsp olive oil or oil

4 garlic cloves, finely chopped

500g (1lb) chicken breasts

1 tsp turmeric

75g (3oz) 1½ cups garlic chives or baby leeks or the green part of spring onions, chopped

50g (2oz) 1 cup parsley, roughly chopped

50g (2oz) 1 cup coriander, finely chopped

15g (½oz) ⅓ cup mint, finely chopped

500–750ml (17–25fl oz) 2–3 cups chicken stock

juice of 1 narenj or Seville orange, or juice of ½ large orange and 1 small lemon, or 125ml (4fl oz) ½ cup verjuice

1 tsp sea salt

few twists of pepper

This is a delicious healthy green dish full of flavour and vitamins. The recipe was kindly given to me by my friend Foad Samiei who owns *Gilac*, a hugely popular restaurant in Tehran serving authentic food from the Caspian region. This recipe normally calls for a whole chicken but Foad uses chicken breasts to cut cooking time, just as I did for my Fesenjan recipe (pomegranate and walnut stew, page 26). He also uses chicken stock to put back some of the flavour lost by not using chicken on the bone.

Boil the split peas for 10 minutes. Drain and set aside.

In a large pan sauté the onion in 1 tbsp oil until light golden. Add the garlic, chicken and turmeric, and cook until the meat is seared but not cooked. Remove to a plate and use the same pan for the next step. Sauté the herbs with the remaining tablespoon of oil on a medium heat and stir frequently for about 5 minutes.

Add the split peas, stir to mix for a minute, then add the chicken and onion mixture along with the stock. Cover and let the whole thing cook for about 45–60 minutes or until the chicken is tender. Add the citrus juices or verjuice and the salt and pepper 10 minutes before the end of the cooking time. Serve this fabulous dish with *kateh* (soft cooked rice, page 109).

ASHEH RESHTEH
NEW YEAR NOODLE SOUP

There is a colloquial Persian saying that 'he or she isn't a soup worth burning your mouth for' (*asheh dahan soozi nist*), but this one really is! It's the mother of all Persian soups, cooked the ancient way in a great big pot and served on special occasions such as funerals, *Nazri* (when food is distributed to the poor) or *Norooz* (Persian New Year's Day). Asheh Reshteh is hearty and full of sustenance, containing spinach, rice noodles (to represent life's many paths), kidney beans and chickpeas, and topped with whey, fried mint and onions.

Every family has their own version. My recipe has lots of onions on top but none in the soup. In the past, people used to add dollops of Gheymeh (meat stew with tomatoes, page 214). Experiment and see which you prefer.

Put all the soaked, drained beans, but not the lentils, in a big pot and cover with the stock or water. Bring to the boil and boil rapidly on a high heat for 10 minutes, skimming if you need to, then lower the heat to medium and cook for about 45 minutes.

Add the lentils and cook for a further 20 minutes. Add the chopped herbs and leaves, turmeric, salt and pepper and let the water come up to the boil again. Cook for around 10 minutes or until there are two bubbles in the middle of the soup – *do ghol*.

At this point, add the noodles, breaking them up with your hands first. Cook for about 20 minutes or so, or until the noodles are done. The cooking time is a little less than average so that the herbs and leaves stay green.

Make the topping by frying the garlic in 1 tbsp oil. Fry the onions separately in another tablespoon of oil until golden and crispy. Fry the mint separately in the remaining oil until dark, stirring all the time otherwise it will burn – about 1 minute. To serve this magical soup, pour into a large bowl, top with fried mint, fried onions and garlic and creamy *kashk* (up to 1 tbsp per person; if it's thick just use ½ tbsp).

TIP: *Kashk* is sold in Middle Eastern food shops. If you can't find any, substitute soured cream, although it will change the taste. For more information on *kashk*, see Kashgeh Bademjan (grilled aubergine spread topped with creamy whey, fried onions and walnuts, page 144).

50g (2oz) ¼ cup each of the following: dried chickpeas, dried red kidney beans, brown lentils, dried haricot beans (*lubia chitti*), soaked overnight then drained

2.25–2.5 litres (3¾–4 pints) 9–10 cups unsalted chicken stock or beef stock or water – enough to cover the beans

25g (1oz) ½ cup garlic chives or spring onions, chopped

50g (2oz) 1 cup flat-leaf parsley, chopped

200g (7oz) about 8 cups chopped fresh spinach

125g (4oz) about 5 cups chopped beetroot leaves (*bargeh choghondar*) or more spinach

1 tsp turmeric

2 tsp salt

pepper

200g (7oz) Persian noodles or any thin flat eggless or Asian rice noodles

For the topping:

5–6 garlic cloves, thinly sliced or finely diced

3 tbsp oil or olive oil

2 large onions, thinly sliced

2 tbsp dried mint

250g (8oz) 1 cup *kashk* (see Tip, left)

BOORANIYEH LABOO
SOFT BEETROOT IN CREAMY YOGURT

500g (1lb) unpeeled beetroots, leaves removed

300g (10oz) 1 cup full-fat or low-fat natural yogurt, with a little Greek or strained yogurt stirred in, if you wish

salt and pepper

In autumn, when Tehran's trees turn golden and orange, the city's street vendors sell roasted beetroots along with char-grilled roasted corn and steamed giant fava (broad) beans in their pods. The smell fills the air, and the beetroots' sweet flesh is warming against chilly autumn days. In the past, people used to pop beetroots, along with potatoes and other root vegetables, to roast in the hot *tanoor*, a giant wood-fired oven used for baking bread.

According to the doctrine of *Unani* (see page 16), beetroot is known for its blood-cleansing qualities. The leaves are also chopped and used in heartier soups such as Asheh Reshteh (New Year noodle soup, page 98). This recipe is one of a series of *booraniyeh* or dips (see also spinach and yogurt dip, page 94). The colour is stunning and it makes a very pretty side salad.

Simply put the unpeeled beetroots in a large pan of water, cover and cook slowly for about 2–2½ hours until a knife goes through them with ease. Let them cool.

Peel the beetroots (wear rubber gloves please!) and chop them into small 2.5cm (1in) cubes. Add the yogurt (I like to mix in a little strained yogurt too), gently mix together and watch the white instantly turn pink. Add salt and pepper to taste.

سالاد شیرازی

SALAD E SHIRAZI
FRESH CRUNCHY CUCUMBER, TOMATO AND ONION SALAD SPRINKLED WITH MINT

4–5 Persian cucumbers or any small compact cucumbers (skin on or peeled, as you wish), chopped into small even-sized cubes

2 large firm but ripe tomatoes, deseeded and chopped into small even-sized cubes

1 large sweet red onion, chopped into small even-sized cubes

2–3 tbsp Middle Eastern red vinegar or juice of 1 fresh lemon

salt and a little pepper, to taste

2 tbsp olive oil

1 tsp dried mint

5–6 fresh mint leaves, finely chopped (optional)

A simple refreshing salad, its vinegary taste marrying well with heavier Persian meals, cutting through any slightly oily stew or rice. Salad e Shirazi resembles a coarse salsa or *pico de gallo* (chunky uncooked Mexican salsa), but it is a salad not a condiment and is served as a side dish to many Iranian rice dishes such as Lubia Polo (page 210).

It is extremely simple to make. Use Persian cucumbers if you can find them, otherwise any compact small ones will do. Since there aren't many ingredients in this recipe, it's best to use the freshest, crunchiest vegetables available. Traditionally, the dressing was made with Middle Eastern red vinegar, which contains no alcohol, but red wine vinegar or lemon juice will do if you can't track any down. Dried mint was used in preference to fresh in the past, but I like to chop some fresh mint leaves along with the dried.

Chopping the vegetables to approximately the same size ensures even distribution of the dressing – and the salad looks prettier. Add the vinegar or lemon juice, salt and pepper, olive oil and mint and mix gently. Serve straight away, as the cucumbers tend to release their juices and become limp over time.

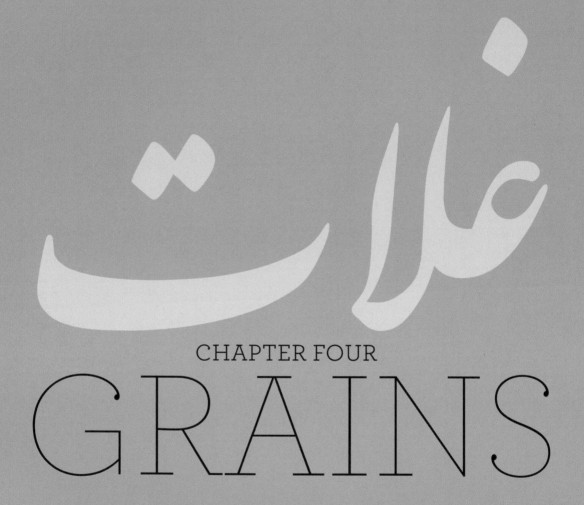

غلات

CHAPTER FOUR
GRAINS

پلو با ته دیک

POLO BA TAADIG

PERFECT FLUFFY RICE
WITH A GOLDEN
CRUST

Iranians take a lot of pride in cooking rice. The recipe
below may make you feel like you're creating a really
complicated dish rather than just plain rice. But, as the
name suggests, it takes plain rice and elevates it to
something special: an elegant aromatic dish that you
would happily eat on its own. Iran grows some of the best
rice in the world. Alas, there isn't enough to export, so
you must pay a visit to savour its wonderful varieties. The
recipe, of course, works just as well with other rice.

600g (1lb 3oz) 3 cups
basmati rice, such as Tilda
or Pari

2 tbsp sea salt

For the taadig:

50–75g (2–3oz) ¼– ⅓ cup
melted butter, ghee or
safflower oil, plus 1 tbsp extra for
the topping

1½ tbsp natural yogurt

¼ tsp saffron threads,
pounded

To decorate:

⅓ tsp saffron liquid,
made from ¼ tsp saffron threads
pounded then dissolved in 1 tbsp
hot water

Fill a large bowl with water and add the rice. Wash the rice by stirring
it with your hands. Pour the water off and repeat 5 times until the
water runs clear. For super-fluffy long-grain rice, soak it in the amount
of water you are going to cook it in – that's 2 litres (3½ pints) 8 cups –
with the salt, for at least 2 hours and up to 24.

Fill a large non-stick pan with 2 litres (3½ pints) 8 cups cold water
and bring to the boil. Add the rice, let the water come to the boil again
and cook for approximately 6–8 minutes. (If you have pre-soaked your
rice, add it to the pan with the cold water, bring to the boil and cook
for 6–8 minutes.) The rice may take a little less or a little more time
depending on the thickness of the pan and the power of the heat, so
test the grains halfway through. Quickly pick out a few grains with a
fork and crush them between your fingers, without burning them. The
grains need to be soft on the outside but still hard on the inside, or al
dente, and they should be double their original size.

While the rice is cooking, stir it ever so gently a couple of times so
that it doesn't stick to the bottom of the pan. The next step is optional
but worth noting: at this point you can add 250ml (8fl oz) 1 cup cold
water to the pan to lengthen the grains. Bring back up to the boil.

Once the rice is cooked, without wasting a minute, drain it through a
very fine-meshed sieve. Pour a couple of cups of cold water over the
rice to cool it and set it aside. Whatever you do, don't touch the rice,
just let it sit there while you move on to the next stage.

In the same pan, briskly heat the melted butter, ghee or oil over a
medium-high heat with 75ml (3fl oz) ⅓ cup water, the yogurt, saffron
and 2 ladles of rice. Mix well and spread over the bottom of the pan to
create the crust. Then start adding the rice a ladleful at a time. Gently
shape the rice into a pyramid as you add it. That way the heat can
circulate throughout the pan and won't make the rice mushy.

Poke 4–5 deep holes in the rice, with a chopstick or the handle of
a spoon, making sure it hits the bottom of the pot, then cover. Let the
rice cook on a high heat for about 5–7 minutes. It will sizzle and make
all kinds of sounds. *Recipe continued on the next page*

POLO BA TAADIG
CONTINUED

Iranian women check to see if the rice is ready for the next step by wetting their fingers and ever so quickly touching the side of the hot pan. If it makes a '*Jez*' sound as we say in Persian, remove the lid and add 125ml (4fl oz) ½ cup water and 1 tbsp butter, ghee or oil. Wrap the lid in a clean tea towel or 2–3 paper towels. Cover the pan, making sure the fabric or paper towel is wrapped up around the handle so that it doesn't catch fire. Reduce the heat to its lowest setting. Allow it to cook for about 50–60 minutes undisturbed.

Fill the kitchen sink with 5cm (2in) of cold water Remove the pan from the stove, and place it in the sink. This helps loosen the famous golden crust or *taadig*. Take the lid off, spoon out a ladleful of rice and mix with the saffron liquid. Gently ladle the rice on to a serving dish and decorate with the saffron rice. Using a spatula, lift chunks of the crust off the bottom of the pan and place on top or serve on the side.

TIP: You can make Polo Ba Taadig in a rice cooker, but make sure it is an Iranian one – other models (for example, Japanese) will not give you long separated grains and a golden *taadig*. Wash 600g (1lb 3oz) 3 cups rice 5 times. Place in the cooker with 900ml (1½ pints) 3½ cups water, the melted butter, ghee or oil, yogurt, and 1 flat tbsp sea salt. Turn the cooker on and gently stir the rice once, after the water has come to the boil, to mix the ingredients together. Cover with a cloth plus lid (see left) and cook for about 1½ hours. Tip the rice on to the serving dish (don't plunge the cooker in cold water). Your rice will come out perfectly, like a golden cake.

BERENJ DOODI
SMOKED RICE

This rice has an unmistakable flavour and aroma because it has been smoked (*dood dadan*). The technique comes from the Gilan and Mazandaran Provinces of Iran near the Caspian sea. The harvested sheaves are hung in a smokehouse over a smouldering mixture of rice chaff and wood or the threshed grains are smoked in containers called *kalevi*. Either way special care is taken so that the grains are left intact. Some people are just wild about smoked rice, while others find it too strong for their liking. I've developed a real addiction to it recently and find it fabulous.

It goes fantastically well with northern dishes such as Fesenjan made with duck (rich pomegranate and walnut stew, page 26). Baghali Ghatogh (broad beans with dill, page 184), Kababeh Torsh (*kabab* marinated in walnuts, pomegranate and garlic, page 158) and Mirza Ghassemi (garlicky smoky aubergines, page 89) are also eaten with it. Traditionally it is not served as a *polo* where rice is mixed with either fruits, meats or nuts. However, I can see this marrying well with non-Persian dishes such as salmon teriyaki, a creamy chicken stew with mushrooms, a shrimp jambalaya or a variety of BBQs. I like to make *kateh* (soft cooked rice, opposite) with it, using lots of butter.

Follow the method for *kateh*, opposite, but soak the rice for at least 8 hours, or better still, 24 hours, beforehand. The grains are harder so a little more oil or butter is needed: add one more tablespoon of oil or butter to the basic recipe.

KATEH
SOFT COOKED RICE

600g (1lb 3oz) 3 cups basmati rice

1 tbsp full-fat natural yogurt (optional)

1 tbsp sea salt

75g (3oz) butter

1 tbsp safflower or other tasteless oil

Kateh is the kind of rice I'm happy to eat all on its own. It's cooked in one pot (with water, butter or oil and salt), so no parboiling and steaming is involved. *Kateh* is usually made at home for lunch or family dinners. It is a little stickier, softer and denser than Polo Ba Taadig (page 106), where the grains are fluffy, long and separated.

In the Caspian region where the rice is grown, *kateh* is eaten in great quantities throughout the day. *Kateh ghalebi* (rice loaf) and *kateh sard* (cold rice) are cut into lozenges and served for breakfast with fish roe and Seer Torshi (aged pickled garlic, page 86) or jam.

There is no need to soak the rice to make *kateh*. Put it in a pan with 1.5 litres (2½ pints) 6 cups water. In Iran we would say that the depth of the water in the pan should be one and a half *bandeh angosht* – which means that, with your index or middle finger touching the top of the rice, the water should reach halfway past the first joint. Add the yogurt and salt and let it boil briskly, uncovered, on a medium-high heat. Stir the rice very gently a couple of times so that the salt and yogurt mix in with the water.

As soon as the water boils away and you see tiny holes appear on the surface of the rice, place knobs of butter evenly across the rice and pour the oil on straight after. I like the combination of both fats, but you can use either/or and adjust the measurements accordingly.

Cover the pan with a lid wrapped in a tea cloth or a few paper towels, making sure the fabric or paper towel is wrapped up around the handle so that it doesn't catch fire. Cook on a very low heat for about 40–45 minutes. Resist the temptation to peek inside. You want to let all that steam do its work.

If your *kateh* ever burns a little at the bottom, remove the pan from the heat, place a piece of plain white spongy bread on top of the rice, cover and leave for 10 minutes. Throw the bread away. This removes some of the burnt smell – a good trick when cooking regular rice too.

Polo Ba Taadig or perfect fluffy rice (page 106),
sprinkled with saffron-infused rice and a pat of butter

FALOUDEH

RICE NOODLE GRANITA
WITH LIME AND
ROSE WATER

100g (3½oz) very thin rice
noodles

850g (1lb 14oz) 3¾ cups
sugar

125ml (4fl oz) ½ cup lime
juice

2 tbsp Persian rose water

lime or lemon wedges,
to serve

Faloudeh is the world's oldest ice cream: a mix of shaved
ice, rice noodles, sugar and rose water. The recipe has
hardly changed since it was created at court 3,000 years
ago and, in Yazd, street vendors still sell it straight from
giant white-copper pots. Their version is less icy and is
served with a wedge of lime to squeeze on top.

This simple recipe is quick to make and is amazing
after a heavy meal; the sharp lime cleanses the palate
yet there's enough sweetness to satisfy your need for a
dessert. Some people add a dollop of Morabayeh Albaloo
(sour cherry jam, page 38) and chopped pistachios.

In Iran, we use rice starch noodles for this recipe but
rice noodles from Asian stores will do. Buy the thinnest
possible, so that they do not become too hard and chunky
when they freeze. I've broken with tradition and added
some fresh lime juice to the mixture.

Boil the rice noodles for a minute in a large pan of hot water. Drain
and pour ice-cold water over them.

Boil the sugar, 500ml (17fl oz) 2 cups water and the lime juice, until
the sugar dissolves, about a minute or so. Let the liquid cool. Add the
noodles and the rose water to the cooled syrup, and churn in an ice-
cream maker. Serve straight away or freeze for later.

If you haven't got an ice-cream maker, pour the mixture into a tray,
freeze for 30 minutes, and fluff the ice with a fork. Repeat twice more
and then let the mixture freeze for a few hours or overnight. This
method will break up the rice noodles considerably, but it's not really
that important. Pile the ice cream high in elegant martini glasses and
serve with lime or lemon wedges.

NAAN E BERENJI

PALE RICE COOKIES
SPRINKLED WITH
POPPY SEEDS

These are beautiful white, melt-in-your-mouth, crumbly cookies sprinkled with black poppy seeds and flavoured with rose water and cardamom. They are traditionally eaten at *Norooz*, the Persian New Year. If you are gluten intolerant you'll be over the moon to discover they are made with rice flour. My grandmother Talat always had these ready for any unexpected guests. I used to buy them for her in a box along with Biscuiteh Keshmeshi (raisin cookies, page 45), which she kept locked in a cupboard. If she didn't keep them under lock and key they would be eaten by the kids within minutes!

Try to make the dough the day before: it really benefits from resting and coming together before baking.

150g (5oz) butter or 150ml (¼ pint) ¾ cup oil

2 small eggs

200g (7oz) 1½ cups icing sugar

1 tsp ground cardamom

2–3 tbsp rose water

100ml (3½fl oz) ⅓ cup safflower or any flavourless oil

500g (1lb) 3½ cups rice flour

1–2 tbsp poppy seeds, to decorate

Take the butter, if using, and eggs out of the fridge about 20 minutes before you begin, so that they are at room temperature. Beat the eggs in a separate bowl and set aside.

Cream the butter, sugar and cardamom in a food processor fitted with a paddle or use a hand-held whisk. Once creamy and fluffy, add the eggs in stages, whisking after each addition. Add the rose water, mix a little, then add the oil and stir. Gently fold in the flour. If you use the food processor to do this stage, do not overmix. Leave the dough in the fridge overnight or for at least 8 hours so it hardens and can be rolled out by hand.

Preheat your oven to 180°C/350°F/Gas Mark 4. Line a baking tray with baking parchment or a Silpat non-stick baking mat. Use a mini ice-cream scoop or a spoon to remove walnut-sized pieces of dough. Roll them into balls and place on the baking tray. Flatten them slightly then either use a fork or the back of a teaspoon to make simple shapes, or press them with a flower-shaped stamp. Sprinkle with the poppy seeds and bake in the oven for about 12–15 minutes.

The most important thing you need to remember is that these cookies will not change colour – they stay white. Remove from the tray and on to cooling racks. Be gentle as they are quite delicate.

YAKH DAR BEHESHT
ICE IN HEAVEN

1 litre (1¾ pints) 4 cups
milk

75g (3oz) ¾ cup rice flour

150g (5oz) ¾ cup sugar,
preferably unrefined

2 tbsp rose water

5 cardamom pods,
lightly crushed

2 tbsp slivered pistachios

noghl, to serve (see page 78)

rose petals and edible gold
leaf, to serve (optional)

I love to serve Yakh dar Behesht after a heavy meal. This delicate Persian custard laced with rose water and sprinkled with pistachios takes me back to a beautiful walled garden in Isfahan. It is traditionally made with milk but for a dairy-free version simply use rice or almond milk instead. Serve in individual ramekins or a large bowl and scatter with rose petals and edible gold leaf. Your guests will be transported to another time and place where desserts are savoured slowly.

Place the milk, rice flour and sugar in a saucepan. Stir constantly with a wooden spoon, over a medium-low heat until the sugar dissolves and the mixture starts to thicken – about 10 minutes. Make sure it doesn't catch at the bottom by scraping the bottom and sides of the saucepan with your spoon.

Add the rose water and the cardamom pods and continue cooking and stirring until the custard is thick and glossy – about another 2 minutes. The custard will resemble a white crème pâtissière.

Pick out the cardamom pods, then pour the custard into ramekins, silicone moulds or a serving dish. Leave to cool in the fridge for a few hours, then sprinkle with slivered pistachios, *noghl* (though this is not traditional), rose petals and gold leaf if using.

کوش فیل

GOOSHEH FEEL

ELEPHANTS' EARS

These delicate fried cookies are one of the first things I ever made, supervised by my *Mamani* (see opposite). They are made from filo pastry and shaped like elephants' ears, and drizzled with rose-flavoured syrup or dusted with icing sugar. The best thing about this recipe is using readymade filo pastry: it cuts down the preparation to a few minutes. Serve with hot tea and enjoy!

safflower, rapeseed
or any other flavourless oil
with a high smoking point

75g (3oz) readymade filo
pastry (about 5 sheets)

For the syrup:

300g (10oz) 1¼ cups sugar

1 tbsp rose water

Make the syrup. In a medium-sized saucepan bring the sugar and 150ml (¼ pint) ½ cup water to the boil and cook on a medium heat for about 15 minutes. Remove from the heat and add the rose water.

Pour the oil into a large saucepan to a depth of about 5–8cm (2–3in). Heat to about 180°C/350°F. To test whether the oil is ready, drop in a piece of pastry: it should bubble up and turn golden gradually without smoking or burning. Have a cooling rack ready.

While the oil is heating, cut out two 8cm (3in) half moons from the filo pastry and pinch the sides to join them together so that they look like a pair of elephant's ears. Do the same with the rest of the pastry. Slide the ears into the hot oil on a spatula and fry until golden. Remove with a slotted spoon. Either place on the rack to cool or immediately dip them into the syrup then place on the rack.

Or instead of dipping them in syrup, let the ears cool before sprinkling generously with icing sugar.

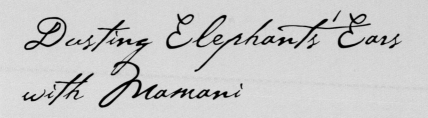

Dusting Elephants' Ears with Mamani

I loved hanging out in the kitchen with my *Mamani* (my grandmother Talat). I could talk to her about anything. She was way ahead of her time, unlike most elderly people I knew. We would chat, have our favourite snack of bread and walnuts with *panir-e-koozeyi* (aged feta cheese) and orange marmalade, with hot tea. She had a long breakfast table in her kitchen and her seat was at the head of that table. No one was allowed to sit in it. If any of us did and she entered the kitchen, she would just nod her head and we'd fly out of the chair as if it were on fire!

The table was set with the usual salt and pepper, as well as olive oil and *serkeh* (vinegar) and bowls of *noghl* (sugared almonds, page 78) and *ajeel* (trail mix, page 68). She also had *ghahoot* (ground almonds or chickpeas mixed with sugar) on top of her fridge, which she would eat spoonfuls of when no one was looking.

She made soups or *ash* in her pressure cooker almost every day, with fresh herbs, lentils, fruits and meat, or whatever she had to hand. When my grandfather was alive, she would put everything in front of him and he would say, 'Bah, bah!' – a Persian expression meaning wow, wonderful or, in this case, yummy.

The most memorable recipe I made with my grandmother was Goosheh Feel (elephants' ears, opposite). These are the cutest of all cookies. They're easy to make with children and powdering them afterwards with icing sugar is so much fun. We would dust them from way up high, like the first snow of the season, the initial layer melting into the pastry and the second gently covering it. We arranged them elegantly in a pyramid and took them to the living room to be served with tea. The rest would keep in a box for ages, since Tehran is so dry they never spoiled. Elsewhere, though, I would put them in a sealed container and possibly in the fridge, but refrain from dusting them until just before serving.

Iran is the last place you would associate with elephants, but in ancient times the Asian elephant with its small ears roamed wild on the plateaus. Elephants were used in battles, notably one between Alexander the Great and Darius III of Persia. However, their numbers dwindled and in time they became extinct.

Chosseh Fil is another food named after the elephant: it's a cheeky term meaning elephant farts! Its proper name is popcorn. When popcorn was introduced to Iran and people ate it for the first time, they were unimpressed, saying that it was like the fart of a great big elephant – in other words, a load of hot air.

FAMILY
MEMOIR

HALVA
DENSE BUTTERY
CONFECTION
WITH ROSE WATER

500g (1lb) 2 cups caster sugar

½ tsp saffron threads, pounded then dissolved in 2–3 tbsp hot water

3 tbsp rose water

300g (10oz) 2 cups plain flour

475g (15oz) 2 cups melted butter or oil

pistachios, to decorate

Most Westerners have tasted *halva* – a mix of pounded sesame seeds and sugar – on holiday in Greece or Turkey. Iranian versions are different as they are made with flour. In the 19th century there were as many as 21 recipes: now just a few survive: *halvayeh ard* (flour), *berenj* (rice flour), *gole zard* (yellow flower), *tar* (wet) and the more familiar *arda* or *halvardeh* (sesame). There is also *kaci*, a thicker, fattier *halva* with added cumin, given to women who have just given birth to help them regain their strength.

Roll up your sleeves: this needs some elbow grease! In a saucepan boil the sugar and 250ml (8fl oz) 1 cup water for about 5 minutes until a thin syrup forms. Add the saffron liquid and rose water and let it sit.

Sift the flour into a frying pan set over a medium-high heat and stir with a wooden spoon until golden in colour. You need to stir it pretty much continuously, so that it doesn't burn, for about 10–15 minutes. This step is important, to remove the raw smell of the flour.

As soon as the flour is golden, add the melted butter or oil to the pan and cook for a further 4–5 minutes, still stirring. Add the syrup, making sure it is warm, not hot. It will sizzle and bubble up. Keep stirring until the mixture absorbs the syrup and starts to form a paste.

Now pick up the pan by its handle and with a rolling motion move the paste from side to side until it sticks together and looks like a sausage. Tip the paste on to a shallow plate and press down with a spoon to spread it evenly. Make indentations with the back of a spoon and scatter some pistachios on top. Leave to cool. If you don't eat it all at once, keep it in the fridge.

نان خامه ای

NOON KHAMEYI
CREAM-FILLED CHOUX BUNS

Iranian pastries have been influenced by French patisserie: *noon khameyis* are a perfect example, as well as being my absolute favourites. Their shell is slightly crisp and when you bite into one you're met with smooth, soft, fluffy, Chantilly whipped cream.

I was very young but I remember *noon khameyis* were served at my paternal grandfather's funeral. I was confused because people were wearing black and in deep mourning, yet they were eating my favourite cream buns. The recipe below is a very step-by-step method, but it isn't difficult at all. You'll never be afraid of choux pastry again. The shells freeze beautifully, too.

For the choux pastry:

5g (¼oz) salt

5g (¼oz) sugar

4 medium eggs, at room temperature

100g (3½oz) unsalted butter, cut into pieces

150g (5oz) 1 cup plain flour

For the egg wash:

1 whole egg plus 3 egg yolks

pinch of sugar

pinch of salt

For the crème Chantilly:

400g (13oz) 1½ cups double cream

100g (3½oz) ¾ cup icing sugar

½ tbsp rose water

Prepare a baking tray lined with either a Silpat non-stick baking mat or silicone paper. Make the pastry. Put the salt and sugar in a small to medium-sized pan with 250ml (8fl oz) 1 cup water. Put it to one side. Break the eggs in a bowl and whisk until mixed.

Add the butter to the water mixture, put the pan on the stove and allow it to come just to the boil. As soon as you have one bubble or two in the middle of the liquid, take the pan off the heat and add the flour all at once. Stir out all the lumps with a wooden spoon, then put the pan back on a medium heat and stir until the dough comes together – about 1 minute. Put the dough into a round bowl to cool.

Once cooled, add the beaten eggs in stages, beating after each addition – use a rubber spatula or use your bare hands as if they're paddles! The dough will look slimy at first but as it absorbs the eggs it becomes shiny and glossy.

Make the egg wash by beating the ingredients with 2 tsp water.

Take a piping bag with a simple 2cm (¾in) nozzle, fill it with the dough and pipe out about 20–25 mini balls, about 2.5–3cm (1–1¼in) in size, or 15–18 medium-sized balls on the baking tray. The technique is to first press out the dough, then twist off, so you get a ball with a knobbly bit at the top. Dip a fork in the egg wash and smooth out that bit.

Place the tray in the oven as soon as possible and cook for about 12–13 minutes for small buns and 15–17 minutes for larger ones – or until golden. Remove from the oven and place them on a rack to cool. Meanwhile, whip the cream with the sugar and rose water until soft to medium peaks form. Keep it in the fridge until ready to assemble the buns. Put the cream in a piping bag with a simple small nozzle. Use the nozzle to push a hole in each choux ball and fill with cream. Arrange on a serving tray and enjoy!

سوپ جو سبک مامی

SOUPEH JO SABKEH MOMY
MY MUM'S BARLEY SOUP

500g (1lb) chicken pieces (drumsticks, breast etc), with skin and on the bone

1 small onion, peeled and quartered

2 celery stalks with leaves

1 whole carrot and 3 large carrots, peeled and cut into approx 8cm (3in) pieces

2 bay leaves

½ tsp turmeric

2 garlic cloves, peeled but left whole

1 large potato, peeled and cut into 8–10cm (3–4in) pieces

100–150g (3½–5oz) ½–¾ cup pearl barley, cooked according to pack instructions, or gluten-free buckwheat flakes

1½ tsp salt

¼ tsp saffron threads, pounded then dissolved in 2–3 tbsp hot water

2 tsp finely chopped flat-leaf parsley

couple of twists of the pepper mill

lemon juice or yogurt, to serve

Just like a typical Middle Eastern mum, my mother was always quick to make a pot of soup at the first sign of the sniffles. You could hear her rummaging in the kitchen, opening cupboards – my mum is a very noisy cook. After we children had a snooze, followed by breathing in eucalyptus steam from a basin with a towel over our heads, the soup was finally ready. She would bring us each a bowl with a wedge of lemon to squeeze over.

I must tell you that my mother's version is different from the usual Persian soup. It isn't thick: it's mainly broth made golden with saffron, a few vegetables here and there, a few slivers of chicken breast, some barley kernels at the bottom and a scattering of chopped parsley. But it is a powerhouse of nutrients. One sip and you knew you were on the road to recovery.

Boil the chicken pieces with 2.5 litres (4 pints) 10 cups water on a high heat for about 10–12 minutes. Skim the broth, then add the onion, celery, whole carrot, 1 bay leaf, the turmeric and garlic, and simmer for about an hour. Skim if necessary. Strain the soup and discard everything but the chicken.

Pour the strained soup back into the pot with the chopped carrots, potato, pearl barley (or buckwheat flakes), salt and saffron liquid and remaining bay leaf, and cook for another 20–30 minutes. Meanwhile, remove the skin and bones and shred the chicken flesh; add a few slivers to the soup (keep the rest for Salad Olivier, page 156) with the parsley and pepper. Use a clean paper towel to dab off any excess oil that has come to the surface. Remove the second bay leaf. Serve with fresh lemon juice or cool yogurt.

My mother aged 18

آش جو

ASHEH JO
BARLEY POTAGE

This is a thick hearty soup or *ash*, with lots of healthy beans, pulses and fresh chopped herbs. *Jo* means barley, which gives this soup a different texture. It's a highly comforting winter dish and a nutritious and delicious vegetarian one if you replace the chicken stock. Traditionally the meat is cooked with the vegetables and herbs then taken out and pounded and returned to the soup to cook for a little longer. This produces a thick soup similar to Halim (creamy lamb or turkey porridge, page 216). You could do this or simply leave the pieces of meat intact.

Place the meat, onions and turmeric in a large saucepan with the stock or the water. Bring to the boil on high, skim and then add the beans, lentils and chickpeas and boil for 10 minutes. Reduce the heat and cook for about 45–50 minutes on a low heat. Don't forget to stir occasionally so that it doesn't catch at the bottom.

Add the barley and cook for another 45–50 minutes.

Add the chopped herbs, spinach and rice, along with the salt and pepper and cook for another 50–60 minutes. Be sure to check the water level and add more if you need to.

Start making the topping by frying the garlic and the onions in 1 tbsp oil until golden and crispy. Then fry the dried mint separately in the remaining oil, until dark, stirring all the time otherwise it will burn – about 1 minute.

Either serve the soup as is, or take out a few ladlefuls of the solids, whizz them in the food processor and add back to the soup. This will give it a richer texture similar to the Halim, but not as stretchy.

Pour the soup into a large bowl, top with fried mint, fried onions and garlic and creamy *kashk* – up to 1 tbsp per person (if the *kashk* is thick then add just ½ tbsp).

300g (10oz) de-boned leg of lamb or beef, cut into 2.5cm (1in) cubes

3 large onions, thinly sliced

½ tsp turmeric

2.5–3 litres (4–5 pints) 10–12 cups unsalted chicken or beef stock or hot water

125g (4oz) ½ cup kidney beans, soaked overnight

100g (3½oz) ½ cup lentils, soaked for about 2 hours

100g (3½oz) ½ cup chickpeas, soaked overnight

200g (7oz) 1 cup pearl barley

50g (2oz) 1 cup fresh coriander, coarsely chopped

25g (1oz) ½ cup fresh dill, coarsely chopped

50g (2oz) 1 cup flat-leaf or curly parsley, coarsely chopped

50g (2oz) 1½ cups fresh spinach

75g (3oz) ⅓ cup rice

2 tsp salt

few twists of pepper

For the topping:

5–6 garlic cloves, thinly sliced or finely diced

2 large onions, sliced thinly

2 tbsp oil

2 tbsp dried mint

kashk, to serve (see page 144) or soured cream if unavailable

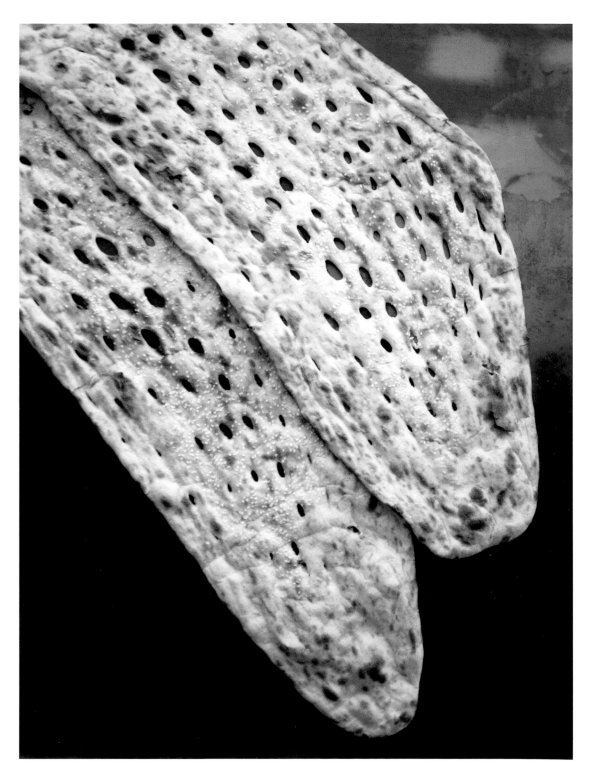

Just add bread to serve with the soup – this is Persian *sangak*

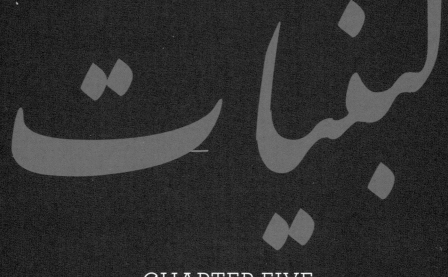

لبنيات

CHAPTER FIVE

DAIRY

دلماج عمو درویش

DOLMAGEH AMOO DARVISH

UNCLE DARVISH'S SALAD OF CHOPPED HERBS, COUNTRY BREAD AND IRANIAN AGED CHEESE

stale *lavash* bread
or pitta bread, lightly toasted

3–4 red radishes, finely sliced
(use a mandoline or a sharp knife),
plus extra to garnish

125g (4oz) ½ cup walnuts,
coarsely chopped, plus extra to
garnish

50g (2oz) 1 cup fresh
herbs such as a mixture
of mint, basil and chives,
roughly chopped, plus extra to
garnish

2–3 spring onions with
stems, roughly chopped

50g (2oz) ½ cup aged
Persian feta or any 'sharp' feta
or mild dry blue cheese

Dolmage is one of those rare dishes that even most Iranians don't know about. My Uncle Darvish, who was a vegetarian, loved this dish and used to carry it in his bag on long walks from one village to another. I hope I will be the first person to introduce you to this recipe as we've enjoyed it in our family for generations. It's a country dish full of fresh herbs, crisp *lavash* bread, chopped walnuts and aged cheese, scattered with thinly sliced radishes. It's a 'hot, sharp' dish (see *Unani*, page 16), eaten for breakfast with hot sweet tea, as a snack or served at parties.

Panir-e-koozeyi is feta cheese that has been aged so that it's similar in taste to blue cheese. My grandmother's servants grated feta from Tabriz (a hard cheese) into terracotta pots. These were sealed and stored in the *ambari* (pantry) for up to a year. Sometimes my grandmother added caraway seeds too. The cheese turns crumbly, rich and sharp, to be used sparingly in Dolmage or eaten with bread, butter, orange jam and walnuts.

Break the bread into bite-sized pieces in a large bowl. Add the radishes, walnuts, chopped herbs and chopped onions, and lastly crumble the cheese on top. Stir the mixture gently with your hands or a spoon and place in a serving dish. Garnish with some more chopped herbs, sliced radishes and walnuts, and serve.

Finely sliced radishes for a country salad

DAIRY 131

NOON PANIR O SABZI KHORDAN
BREAD, FETA AND HERBS

fresh herbs such as: mint, tarragon, basil, garlic chives

spring onions

red radishes

fresh walnuts or dried walnuts soaked in cold water in the fridge (at least overnight) to rehydrate

panir (Persian feta)

fresh noon (bread) such as lavash, barbari, sangak, taftoon or any bread you have handy (Indian naan is a good substitute)

Dairy products are a significant part of the Iranian diet, thanks to the ancient nomadic lifestyle of the people of the plains. Milk and yogurt are most important, cheese less so – hence the limited variety, except for *panir* (feta). *Panir* is a Persian word and Persian *panir* is different from its Indian namesake. Indian *paneer* is harder, so it can be used in stews while still keeping its shape. Persian *panir* can be creamy or crumbly and is never cooked.

This dish is an ideal starter and generally on the menu in Iranian restaurants. It is a 'hot and cold' combination (see *Unani*, page 16): the digestive herbs cleanse the palate and are said to increase appetite. Some people like to end their meals with Noon Panir o Sabzi Khordan, too.

Arrange herbs, onions, radishes, walnuts, cheese and bread on a lovely platter and serve.

PANIR O HENDEVANEH
FETA AND WATERMELON

Watermelon is quintessentially associated with summer in Iran. Children eat vast quantities and there is always one in the house to cut open when guests arrive on a hot day. People sometimes put them to cool in the swimming pool or in shallow streams. Watermelons are usually eaten as a fruit or in juice form and rarely incorporated in recipes, except for the following dish – which isn't really a dish so much as a snack, so no recipe needed. It's something that people used to eat in olden times and it's still a favourite with labourers as it's inexpensive and refreshing.

Despite that, you can make it look fancy and serve bread, feta and watermelon on giant platters at parties – the contrast in colour is pretty. The combination of juicy watermelon and salty, slightly crumbly and creamy *panir* cheese is unique. If you cannot find Persian *panir*, use a French brand of feta called Valbreso, made from sheep's milk.

ته چین

TAACHIN
YOGURT AND
GARLIC MARINATED
CHICKEN IN A
SAFFRON RICE CAKE

Taachin means 'to arrange everything at the bottom'. This is a savoury cake that's perfect for parties for its stunning visual effect. It's ideal for picnics too, as it's easy to transport. Rice is layered with chicken marinated with yogurt and garlic and lots of saffron. There's also a lamb and spinach version, as well as one layered with aubergine, which is a fairly 'new' recipe. You could also stud the rice with barberries as in Zereshk Polo (rice with chicken, saffron and barberries, page 42). For parties just prepare it in advance and put in the oven at the last minute – the presentation is guaranteed to impress.

There is much debate in our family as to whether onions and egg yolks should be included or not. I decided to do the version that I like best, with both onions and egg yolks.

800g (1lb 10oz) 4 cups basmati rice, soaked in water for at least 5 hours

500–600g (1–1¼lb) skinless, boneless, chicken breasts, cut into 8cm (3in) cubes

2 tbsp unsalted butter

1 tbsp olive oil

1 medium white onion, chopped

½–1 tsp salt

few twists of pepper

½ tsp turmeric

6–7 small garlic cloves, peeled and diced

1kg (2lb) 4 cups Greek yogurt

½ tsp saffron threads, pounded then dissolved in 2–3 tbsp hot water

75g (3oz) 1 cup dried barberries (optional)

4 egg yolks

Cook the rice till *al dente*; follow the method for Polo Ba Taadig (perfect fluffy rice, page 106) up to draining and cooling.

Place the chicken, butter, oil, onion, some salt and pepper, turmeric and half of the garlic in a large frying pan. Cover and cook for about 30 minutes on a low heat. Tip the mixture into a bowl and cool for 10–15 minutes. Add the yogurt, the rest of the garlic and saffron liquid: mix well. Marinate in the fridge for at least 2 hours, or overnight.

If using barberries, wash them as for Zereshk Polo (page 42).

Preheat the oven to 190°C/375°F/Gas Mark 5. Take the chicken out of the marinade and set aside. Add the egg yolks to the marinade mixture with some extra salt and stir well. Then take the cooked rice and set aside 175g (6oz) 1 cup for later. Ladle the remainder of the rice into the yogurt and egg mixture. Fold it in, but be gentle so that the rice grains don't get crushed, otherwise you'll be left with a mushy cake. Stop as soon as the whole thing is amalgamated.

Take a non-stick baking dish and spread the reserved cup of plain rice over the bottom. Then add a third of the rice and egg mixture. Layering the dish in this way stops the rice and egg mixture coming into direct contact with the pan and burning. Add a layer of chicken pieces (and barberries if using) then a layer of rice again. Repeat until the dish is filled. Cover with a lid if it has one or wrap with foil. Place in the oven and cook for 1½ hours until the bottom is golden brown. When the dish is cooked, invert it over a plate immediately, so that the crunchy *taadig* (crust) at the base doesn't go soggy.

MAST O KHIAR
COLD CUCUMBER SOUP WITH PLUMP RAISINS, WALNUTS, MINT AND SPRING ONIONS

1 large cucumber,
semi peeled, seeded and diced
or 6 small cucumbers, diced

400g (13oz) 1½ cups low-fat
Greek yogurt or crème fraîche

200g (7oz) ¾ cup full-fat
natural yogurt

200g (7oz) ¾ cup soured
cream

50g (2oz) ½ cup raisins

4 tbsp roasted walnuts,
chopped

1 tbsp chopped fresh mint

½ tsp dried mint

3 tarragon sprigs, finely
chopped

2 spring onions,
finely chopped

1 tsp sea salt

fresh pepper, to taste

1 tsp dried rose petals,
to decorate

Iranians eat a lot of cucumbers. They're considered more of a fruit than a vegetable and eaten as such. The cucumbers in Iran are small, juicy and packed with flavour. When you bite into one, the smell fills the whole room. At parties, they're piled high, with some rock salt on the side for sprinkling.

This yogurt and cucumber soup is an example of a perfectly balanced 'hot' and 'cold' dish (see *Unani*, page 16): 'cold' yogurt is mixed with 'hot' walnuts and raisins, with fresh herbs for easy digestion.

Here, I've used different types of yogurts to mimic the texture and slightly sour taste of yogurt made in the villages of Iran. You can also use just natural full-fat or even fat-free yogurt, mixed with a teaspoon of lemon juice. One of my best foodie friends Maryam Samiy uses champagne grapes (see page 45) instead of raisins, which adds a whole new dimension to this dish.

Mix all the ingredients except the rose petals together in a large bowl. But if preparing in advance, add the cucumbers at the last minute so that they stay crunchy and don't give out too much juice. You can also slice the cucumber first, sprinkle with salt, leave for an hour in a colander, run under the tap to remove the excess salt, dry the slices and then dice them. They'll be extra crunchy and will not go limp the next day in case you have any soup left over.

Sprinkle the soup with rose petals and serve in individual bowls. On a hot day, add a few ice cubes.

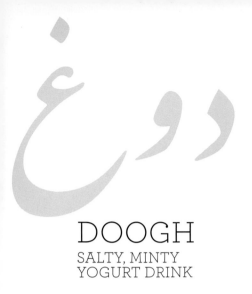

DOOGH
SALTY, MINTY
YOGURT DRINK

300g (10oz) 1 cup Greek yogurt or kefir

75ml (3fl oz) ⅓ cup mineral water, sparkling or still

3 sprigs of fresh mint, very finely chopped, or a pinch of dried mint

⅓ tsp salt, or more depending on your taste

twist of pepper (optional)

This is a yogurt drink that is faintly soured, speckled with mint, and a little salty and fizzy. I make it with carbonated water rather than following the traditional method of leaving it at room temperature for around two days to ferment slightly. Commercially made *doogh* contains soda water, which you could also use – or use plain tap water if you don't want the fizz. It is a refreshing drink on a hot day – and is also served with the famous Chelo Kabab (kneaded *kabab*, page 148).

Doogh comes from the Persian verb *doushidan*, which means 'to milk' and has been recorded as far back as the 11th century, when it was made by shaking milk in a sheepskin. I like making it with Greek yogurt because it has a slightly sour note to it. Kefir, which is similar to probiotic yogurt, is another great healthy option. Simply whisk all the ingredients together and serve with ice.

كیک مامانی طلعت

CAKEH MAMANI
GRANDMOTHER'S YOGURT CAKE

I'll never forget the smell of my grandmother's yogurt cake: the aroma would fill the air. The golden cake rose in the middle and cracked, and the crust was ever so slightly crunchy and chewy at the same time.

My grandmother got the recipe from her piano teacher's wife Mrs Bobkin, an Armenian-Iranian violinist. My mum told me that when she and my aunt were little, my grandmother wouldn't give them any sweets or cakes for a few days before her piano lesson. Then, when they went with her, she would give them each a slice of yogurt cake – they were so thrilled that they didn't mind the long wait outside the classroom so much.

Similar in texture to a pound cake, it is one of the first things Iranians learn to bake. I sometimes like to add walnuts, raisins or blueberries, or even chocolate chips, or spread it with jam or cream cheese.

300g (10oz) 2 cups plain flour

1½ tsp baking powder

½ tsp bicarbonate of soda

tiniest pinch of salt

250g (8oz) 1 cup sugar, caster or granulated

zest of ½ lemon

2 medium eggs, at room temperature

75g (3oz) melted butter or safflower or olive oil

300g (10oz) 1 cup full-fat natural yogurt

1 tsp pure vanilla extract

Preheat the oven to 180°C/350°F/Gas Mark 4. Prepare a 22cm (9in) non-stick cake tin by rubbing it with butter, especially the edges.

In a large bowl sift the flour with the baking powder, bicarbonate of soda and salt. In another bowl, whisk the sugar with the lemon zest for a few seconds. This will release the oils from the zest. Add the eggs and whisk for about 3–4 minutes with an electric beater. Next whisk in the melted butter or oil, yogurt and vanilla extract, switching to a spatula halfway through and folding the batter until just mixed. Do not overbeat. Pour the batter into the cake tin and bake for about 30–35 minutes or until a skewer or sharp knife inserted in the middle comes out clean. Resist the temptation to peek!

Once the cake is golden and ready, leave it in the tin for about 5 minutes to rest a little and shrink for easier removal – don't leave it any longer as the cake will then steam and become gooey. Flip the tin over and invert the cake on to a cooling rack. This cake is best eaten at room temperature. So please wait and don't do what I've just done – I ate a piece straight away and burned the roof of my mouth.

A Big Fat Persian Wedding

The movie *My Big Fat Greek Wedding* made a lot of us Iranians laugh out loud at the similarities between our cultures. My own wedding was not unlike the movie, with my Welsh husband's small and slightly reserved family looking on bemusedly at the antics of my large, exuberant clan.

Persian weddings are big and colourful, with a host of ceremonies and rituals, starting with the courtship itself. People tend to marry from the same background in terms of money, family, even business. This is less the case now in big cities, although Iranians believe that marriages last longer when the in-laws know each other or, preferably, are distantly related. Arranged marriages still occur in rural areas or in very traditional families. This practice was never as important or as strictly followed as in India or Pakistan. However, family consent on both sides is paramount. In ancient times astrologers were consulted for an auspicious date for the wedding – now it's just at everyone's convenience.

The Iranian marriage is made up of the *Aghd* (tying the knot) and the actual wedding celebration or *Aroussi*. The former is the legal part of the ceremony. A *Mehrieh*, or ransom, is also agreed – a fixed price for the bride's financial security in case of divorce. It can be gold coins, land or even *yek chagheh nabat* – one sugar crystal – to show that they are not interested in money.

Three days before the wedding, the bride is taken to the beauty salon for waxing or threading (*band andazy*) – depilation treatments – and her eyebrows are plucked. This used to be a rite of passage but now many city women do this before they are married. The day before, the bride goes to a *hammam* (steam bath) where she is scrubbed (*kisseh keshi*) with a loofah and massaged with fragrant oils.

The *Aghd* ceremony dates back to Zoroastrian times. A room in the bride's house is decorated with flowers and a large *sofreh* (tablecloth) is placed on the floor or on a large low table in the direction of the sunlight to reflect the Zoroastrian duality of darkness versus light. The *sofreh* is decorated with a mirror; two candelabras symbolising light and fire; sugar and honey for a sweet life; *esfand* (incense) to ward off the evil eye; gold coins for prosperity; and eggs and wheat for fertility.

The bride and groom sit side by side, looking at each other only through the mirror while the priest or mullah gives the blessings.

The groom says his 'I do's' but tradition dictates that the bride should be coy initially, when asked for her consent. Friends cry out, 'She has gone to pick flowers' or 'She is thinking'; only on the third time of asking does she say 'I do!' The relieved groom then places a ring on her finger and she on his, and they finish by dipping their little fingers in honey and putting them in each other's mouths.

Guests give them gold coins, money and jewellery, then shower them with *noghl* (sugared almonds, page 78) and rice as they leave the room.

FAMILY
MEMOIR

Candelabras
symbolise fire
and light at a
Persian wedding

كشك بادمجان

KASHGEH BADEMJAN

GRILLED AUBERGINE
SPREAD TOPPED
WITH CREAMY WHEY,
FRIED ONIONS,
GARLIC, MINT AND
WALNUTS

6–7 medium aubergines

60ml (2½fl oz) ¼ cup olive
oil, extra virgin or regular

1 large onion, thinly sliced

4 garlic cloves, finely chopped

75g (3oz) ¼ cup *kashk*

½ tsp salt

pepper, to taste

For the topping:

2 sprigs of fresh mint,
finely chopped or 1 tsp dried mint

2 tbsp olive oil, plus extra
to drizzle

2 garlic cloves, finely chopped

3 tbsp *kashk*

⅓ tsp saffron threads,
pounded then dissolved in 2 tbsp
hot water

1 tbsp ground walnuts

Kashk gives this rich aubergine dish its special edge. It is dried buttermilk – a by-product of cheese-making that is either compressed into round balls (see photograph, page 129) or powdered. Before adding to dishes it must be mixed with water to create a paste or liquid whey. *Kashk* has depth of flavour – think liquid feta but much stronger in taste and with the consistency of *tahini*. Ready-mixed *kashk* is conveniently sold in jars in Persian food shops.

Kashgeh Bademjan is generally served at parties as an appetiser with lots of thin *lavash* bread for dipping.

Bake the whole aubergines at 200°C/400°F/Gas Mark 6 for 45–60 minutes until charred. Remove the skin, chop the flesh and place in a non-stick frying pan with the olive oil and onion, and fry until golden. Add the chopped garlic at the very end and allow it to brown. Then add just enough water to cover the mixture and let it simmer for about 20–30 minutes so that it becomes soft enough to purée.

Purée the cooked aubergine and onion mixture in a food processor, with a hand-held mixer, pestle and mortar or even a potato masher, along with the *kashk*, plus salt and pepper to taste.

Make the topping. Fry the mint in 1 tbsp oil, and set aside. Fry the garlic in the remaining oil until golden, then set aside.

Spread the aubergine purée on a large shallow plate. Garnish with the fried mint and garlic, the *kashk* and a drizzle of olive oil and saffron liquid. Sprinkle with walnuts and serve with *lavash* bread or any other thin bread, although a crusty baguette will also do nicely.

For a quick version, instead of baking whole aubergines, cut them into 8cm (3in) cubes. Place in a colander, run a little water over and then salt them to sweat away the bitterness. After 20–30 minutes, wipe the pieces with paper towels, then follow the method above.

TIP: To serve the purée as in the photograph, halve 2 large or 4 medium aubergines and scoop out the flesh. Wrap the shells in foil and bake for 20 minutes at 190°C/375°F/Gas Mark 5. Remove the foil and cook the shells for another 5–10 minutes so that they dry out a bit. Fill with the purée, decorate and serve.

CHAPTER SIX

MEAT

CHELO KABAB
KNEADED KABAB

500g (1lb) fatty ground lamb or beef, ask your butcher to mince it twice or mince it again when you get home

¼ tsp turmeric

generous pinch of baking powder

salt and pepper, to taste

1 medium onion, grated and liquid drained off

melted butter, for basting

cherry tomatoes

sumac powder, to serve

basil or herbs, to serve

lavash bread or thin naan, to serve

Chelo Kabab is the national dish of Iran. It can be marinated grilled mutton or pieces of ground meat. Either way, it is served with a pyramid of saffron-flavoured buttery fluffy rice, char-grilled tomatoes, purple sumac powder to combat the heaviness of the meat and for better digestion (see *Unani*, page 16), and a side of *torshi* (pickles, page 84). Sometimes fresh onions, raw egg yolks, *torshiyeh ambeh* (mango relish) and sweet basil are served as accompaniments. *Doogh*, the salty minty yogurt drink (page 138), is traditionally served with Chelo Kabab.

The combination of dairy, carbs and meat makes this dish unique and highly nutritious. It also makes you sleepy straight afterwards – which is why it is best eaten at the weekend when not much is required of you.

This *kabab* needs a fair amount of kneading. Knead the meat, turmeric, baking powder, salt and pepper and grated onion, until you have a sticky paste. In a food processor this takes a matter of moments. In Iran the butcher minces the meat with onions three times until it becomes almost white. The mixture needs to be sticky so that the meat actually sticks to the skewers – and to make sure that the end result is smooth and fine.

Either grill the *kababs* on a barbecue or put them under a hot grill for a quick lunch. If grilling the *kababs*, you won't need skewers. Simply roll the *kababs* into sausage shapes around 20cm (8in) long, then place on a roasting tray covered with foil. (Have a bowl of cold water while you're working and dampen your hands so the meat doesn't stick to them.) Use a fork to mark the tops with little ridges.

Preheat the grill on high. Brush the *kababs* with a little melted butter and grill for 4–5 minutes on one side. Flip over, baste again and grill for another 3–4 minutes or until the outside is char-grilled and slightly scorched but the inside is tender and moist. Grill a few cherry tomatoes alongside.

Sprinkle with sumac and serve with Polo Ba Taadig (perfect fluffy rice, page 106) or *kateh* (soft cooked rice, page 109), Torshiyeh Liteh (pickled aubergines, page 187) and a plate of fresh sweet basil or Sabzi Khordan (fresh herbs, page 132). If there is any juice left in the pan, don't forget to pour it on your rice. Or eat the *kababs* with herbs, wrapped inside *lavash* or plain *naan* bread. At a barbecue offer guests a mixture of *kababs*, including Joojeh Kabab (chicken *kabab*, page 154), pictured opposite.

GIGOT
ROAST LEG OF LAMB
WITH SAFFRON
AND YOGURT

1½–2kg (3–4lb) leg of lamb

7 garlic cloves, cut in half
if large, plus 2 garlic bulbs

1 small carrot, cut into
thin rings

4 tbsp olive oil

1 large onion, thinly sliced

5 tbsp natural yogurt

½ tsp saffron threads,
pounded then dissolved in
2–3 tbsp hot water

2 tsp turmeric

2 tbsp Dijon mustard
(optional, as it is not very Persian!)

1 tbsp salt

few twists of pepper

2 bay leaves

2–3 generous tbsp butter

Throughout the country Iranians prefer lamb to beef
(except in the Caspian region). The sweet grass of the
great Persian plateaus produces delicious lamb. Unlike
lamb reared elsewhere in the world, most of the fat is
stored in the tail of the sheep – so the meat doesn't smell
as strongly because of its lower fat content.

There are many elaborate recipes for lamb, such as
stuffed whole lamb and shoulder stuffed with spices, fruits
and nuts. But I've decided to show you the kind of lamb
we ate at home, which is similar to a Western roast, in the
hope that it will bring our cultures closer together.
We ate this once a week so my mother really perfected
her recipe! I'd get so excited when I'd open the fridge to
find a leg of lamb marinating in yogurt, garlic and spices.

With the tip of a sharp knife, make small incisions in the meat and
insert ½ clove of garlic into each one and press down. Do the same
with the carrot rings. Mix together the olive oil, onion, yogurt, saffron
liquid, turmeric, mustard if using, salt and pepper and spread it on
the lamb. Place in an ovenproof dish, cover and leave in the fridge
overnight or for up to 2 days to marinate.

Heat the oven to 180°C/350°F/Gas Mark 4. Take out the lamb about
30 minutes before cooking, so that it comes to room temperature.

Remove and discard the onions from the marinade. Tuck the bay
leaves into incisions in the meat. Cook the lamb with the bulbs of
garlic in a heavy ovenproof dish for about 1½ hours, covered with
either the lid or foil. Baste occasionally.

Remove the foil and scatter pieces of butter over the lamb. If you
like your meat medium, remove the lamb at this point, otherwise you
need to cook it for another 30 minutes. Then remove the roast, cover
with foil and let it rest for about 20–30 minutes before carving.

My mum served this with either a vegetarian Khoreshteh Esfenaj
(spinach and plum stew, page 92) or roast potatoes.

DOLMEYEH FELFEL

STUFFED PEPPERS WITH
RICE, GROUND LAMB, FRESH
HERBS AND SPLIT PEAS

Dolmehs are spectacular served on a large tray – they look beautiful and smell divine. The stuffing is usually a mixture of rice, split peas, ground lamb, onions, a medley of chopped herbs, and turmeric. Sometimes crushed walnuts or barberries are added.

The sauce *dolmehs* are cooked in can be either salty or sweet and sour, depending on the region the recipe comes from and also how the family prefers it. I've given you a recipe for both, so you can choose. Grape molasses or a mixture of lemon juice and sugar can also be used for the sauce.

First make the stuffing. Place the soaked split peas in a saucepan, cover with fresh water and cook for about 30 minutes on a medium-high heat, making sure they are always covered with water.

Meanwhile, sauté the onion in 1 tbsp oil until light gold. Add the meat and continue to cook until the meat is golden. Add the turmeric, stir, then add the tomato purée and continue stirring for a minute or so. Add the salt, pepper and cooked split peas; stir, then add 375ml (13fl oz) 1½ cups water and simmer until the water has evaporated.

Now add the rice and chopped herbs. Stir to mix, remove from the heat and leave to cool.

Prepare the peppers by cutting off and reserving the tops and removing the seeds and membrane. Fill each one with the rice mixture, pressing it down but leaving a little room for expansion. Replace their 'hats'. Pour the remaining oil in a clean saucepan and stand the peppers in the pan vertically, side by side.

Make the savoury sauce by simply mixing the ingredients with 500ml (17fl oz) 2 cups water. Make the sweet and sour sauce by boiling all the ingredients together for about 10 minutes.

Pour your chosen sauce over the stuffed peppers, cover the pan and let it cook on a high heat for about 3–4 minutes, then reduce to the lowest setting and let it cook gently for about 1½–2 hours.

125g (4oz) ½ cup yellow split peas, soaked overnight and drained

1 large onion, finely chopped

2 tbsp oil or olive oil

400g (13oz) ground lamb

½ tsp turmeric

2 tbsp tomato purée

1½ tsp salt

few twists of pepper

200g (7oz) 1 cup rice, soaked for about 2 hours or boiled for 5 minutes and drained

50g (2oz) 1 cup each of fresh coriander, parsley, finely chopped

25g (1oz) ½ cup fresh dill, finely chopped

15g (½oz) ⅓ cup mixture of fresh tarragon, marjoram and mint, finely chopped

7 sweet peppers

For the savoury sauce:

1½ tbsp tomato purée

1 tsp salt

⅓ tsp saffron threads, pounded then dissolved in 2–3 tbsp hot water

For the sweet and sour sauce:

125g (4oz) ½ cup sugar

125ml (4fl oz) ½ cup vinegar such as white wine or cider vinegar

1 tbsp tomato purée

⅓ tsp salt

⅓ tsp saffron threads, pounded then dissolved in 2–3 tbsp hot water

جوجه کباب

JOOJEH KABAB

JUICY CHICKEN KABAB
WITH SAFFRON,
BUTTER AND LEMON

2 medium onions

1 tbsp olive oil

½ tsp saffron threads, pounded then dissolved in 2–3 tbsp hot water

125ml (4fl oz) ½ cup lemon juice

¾ tbsp salt

few twists of pepper

1kg (2lb) chicken pieces, boneless, cut into cubes

100g (3½oz) melted butter

lemon juice (optional)

lavash bread or *naan*, to serve

fresh basil, to serve

sumac powder, to serve

Iranians are famous throughout the Middle East for their deliciously tender and tasty *kababs*. I think that's because they really take their time and make them succulent by letting them marinate well. The marinade has to be special: lots of saffron, lemon juice and sometimes yogurt, so that it sinks into the meat. I'll never forget those late afternoons when the coals were lit for the *kababs*. We would be eating our *mazzes* (appetisers) but knew that in a couple of hours there would be a giant tray of succulent meat on a layer of *lavash* bread soaking up all the lovely juices. In fact, there is a well-known Persian saying: 'You are the bread beneath my *kabab*.'

Grate the onions in a large bowl. Next add the olive oil, saffron liquid, lemon juice, salt and pepper, and mix so that you get a gorgeous yellow lemony mixture. Add the cubed chicken and rub the meat with the marinade. Wear rubber gloves otherwise you'll never be able to get rid of the onion smell from your fingers. Place in the fridge for a minimum of 4 hours and up to 2 days. (You can make the marinade with sliced onions but grated onions are less likely to catch fire on the barbecue and their flavour really seeps into the meat. The marinade is great for regular barbecued chicken portions, too.)

Remove the meat from the marinade. Add the melted butter to the marinade and set aside to use as a basting sauce. If you think you don't have enough sauce, simply add a little lemon juice to it.

Prepare the barbecue or heat the grill to high. Thread the chicken on skewers. Grill for about 3–5 minutes on each side, depending on the thickness of the meat and on how hot the barbecue or grill is. Baste occasionally.

Serve with rice (*polo*, page 106 or *kateh,* page 109) or in between pieces of *lavash* bread with fresh basil and sprinkled with sumac powder. (Photograph on page 149.)

Basil, sumac and onions for *kababs*

سالاد الویه

SALAD OLIVIER
CHICKEN SALAD WITH POTATOES, EGGS, GHERKINS AND PEAS

500g (1lb) chicken breasts on the bone, skin on

1 large onion, roughly chopped

2 bay leaves

250g (8oz) 1 cup mayonnaise

150g (5oz) ½ cup natural yogurt or crème fraîche or soured cream

½ tbsp Dijon mustard

juice of 1 large lemon or 1½ limes

1½ tbsp white wine vinegar or mild cider vinegar

2 tbsp flat-leaf parsley, finely chopped

3 spring onions or 10–12 chives, finely chopped

2 tbsp olive oil

1½ tsp salt

few twists of pepper

1 large potato, cooked, peeled and cut into 5cm (2in) cubes

75g (3oz) ½ cup cooked peas, fresh or frozen

10–12 shop-bought Iranian pickles or gherkins, roughly chopped into 1cm (½in) cubes

2–3 sprigs of fresh tarragon, or ½ tsp dried

4 large eggs, hard-boiled and peeled

Originally from Russia, this dish has been adopted by Iranians as their own. It is one of those simple yet fantastic meals. It's also sold in supermarkets now, but Iranians prefer to make it at home because then they know exactly what's underneath all that mayonnaise. The combination of cooked chicken, peas, lemon juice, mayo, potatoes, eggs and pickles may seem very 1970s kitsch, but it's delicious. People take this salad on picnics, put it in lunch boxes layered between bread and tomatoes, and even serve it all dressed up as an appetiser at parties. Our family version has less mayo and is not so mashed up.

Cook the chicken on a very low heat in 125ml (4fl oz) ½ cup water along with the chopped onion and bay leaves until soft – about 45–60 minutes. Reserve the liquid for another dish, take the flesh off the bones and discard the skin and bones. Leave the chicken to cool then chop it into 2.5cm (1in) cubes.

In a large bowl, add the mayo and yogurt (or crème fraîche or soured cream), mustard, lemon or lime juice, vinegar, chopped parsley, spring onions or chives and olive oil. Season and mix well.

Add the cooked potato, chicken, cooked peas, pickles and tarragon, and fold in until well mixed, mashing it a bit along the way. Roughly chop the eggs and fold them in too. If the salad needs to be a bit creamier, resist adding more yogurt or mayo – add a spoonful of the reserved chicken stock instead.

كباب ترش

KABABEH TORSH

TENDER KABAB
MARINATED IN
GROUND WALNUTS,
POMEGRANATE PASTE
AND GARLIC

1.5kg (3lb) fillet of beef,
cut into strips

For the marinade:

1 large onion,
finely grated

125ml (4fl oz) ½ cup
pomegranate juice

75ml (3fl oz) ⅓ cup
pomegranate paste

3–4 garlic cloves

75g (3oz) 1 cup walnuts,
finely ground

2 tbsp olive oil

salt and pepper

This dish comes from Gilan, an area by the coast of the Caspian sea, where there are lush forests, beautiful rice paddies and olive groves. It was also the last place in Iran to be converted to Islam. People in this region have a different diet to the rest of the country. They eat a lot of garlic, and flavours are fresher, with herbs, citrus and the liberal use of olive oil. This *kabab* recipe is a perfect example. Whereas other recipes use lemon juice, saffron or yogurt in marinades, here the Gilanis have created a special blend of crushed walnuts, pomegranate paste, garlic, olive oil and parsley.

It's almost impossible for the novice cook to prepare meat like a professional *kabab zan* (kabab maker), so use fillet of beef cut into thick strips to get a similar effect. *Kabab zan* specialise in cutting the meat a certain way and putting the pieces on skewers. It really is an art form and it takes many years of training.

Place the marinade ingredients in a bowl and mix together with a splash of water. Add the beef and gently rub the marinade into the meat. Cover and leave to marinate in the fridge for 3–4 hours or overnight, but no longer.

Heat the barbecue until hot or preheat the grill to high. Take the meat out of the fridge at least 30 minutes before cooking to bring it up to room temperature. Remove some of the marinade with a spoon or clean paper towel and thread the meat on to skewers. Grill for 3 minutes on each side for medium-rare *kababs* or 4–5 minutes for medium to well done. Serve with rice (*polo*, page 106 or *kateh*, page 109), Sabzi Khordan (fresh herbs, page 132) and Seer Torshi (aged pickled garlic, page 86).

PERSIAN MACARONI
STEAMED PASTA WITH
A GOLDEN CRUST

ماکارونی

Italians would go mad if they knew what Iranians are doing to their beloved pasta! This dish is a perfect example of how obsessed Iranians are with steaming and slow cooking. Pasta is mixed with Bolognese sauce and the two steamed together to create a soft delightful comfort food. Iranians don't understand the concept of *al dente*. Everything must be cooked well otherwise you might get a stomach ache.

Ironically, pasta may have originated in Persia, even though very little is consumed today. Arab traders spread pasta throughout the rest of the world. *Laksa* in Malay and Indonesian and *lapsha* in Russian, both types of noodle come from the Persian *lakhsha* or 'slippery'. Most Iranians are brought up on this dish. Adding potatoes helps it form a delicious *taadig* (crust).

Make the sauce by first sautéing the onion, garlic, celery, carrot and bay leaves with the oil. Add the ground beef, salt and pepper and turmeric, and cook until brown. Add the tomato purée and stir briefly before adding the fresh or canned tomatoes. Stir, cover, lower the heat and let the sauce cook gently for about 45 minutes. Season well.

Meanwhile, cook the pasta in salted water until *al dente*. Drain, then run a cup of lukewarm water over it to remove some of the starch. Add the pasta to the sauce and mix well until well coated. It may look as though there is too much sauce but don't worry, the pasta will soak it all up.

Wash the pasta pan or use another heavy non-stick pan, and add the butter or oil to the bottom. Heat until it is bubbly but not coloured. Place the sliced potatoes on the bottom, then add the pasta mixture. Cook on a medium-high heat for about 5 minutes, then reduce the heat, place a lid wrapped in a cloth on top and let it cook slowly for about 45–60 minutes.

1 medium onion, finely chopped

2 garlic cloves, finely chopped

1 celery stalk, finely chopped

½ carrot, finely chopped

2 bay leaves

2 tbsp olive oil

500g (1lb) ground beef

1 tsp salt

few twists of black pepper

⅓ tsp turmeric

2 tbsp tomato purée

5–6 large tomatoes, skinned and roughly chopped or 2½ x 400g cans of chopped tomatoes

500g (1lb) spaghetti or penne

1 tbsp butter or 1 tbsp olive oil

1 large potato, sliced (enough to cover the base of the pan)

COTELETTES
MEAT AND
POTATO PATTIES WITH
SAFFRON

2 medium potatoes, cooked, cooled and peeled

10cm (4in) piece of raw potato

375g (12oz) ground beef

1 medium onion, grated and liquid drained off

½ tsp turmeric

tiniest pinch of saffron threads, pounded then dissolved in ½ tbsp hot water (optional)

½ tsp salt

¼ tsp pepper or a few twists of the pepper mill

1 large egg

125g (4oz) 2 cups fine breadcrumbs or gluten-free breadcrumbs

up to 125ml (4fl oz) ½ cup any good-quality flavourless oil

lavash bread or thin naan, to serve

sliced tomatoes, to serve

pickled gherkins, to serve

Cotelettes are meat patties and not, as the name suggests, lamb cutlets. Think hamburgers but made with potatoes and breadcrumbs. Iranians of Turkish descent (as is part of my family) make the best ones. Some families like them thin, others prefer them chunkier. Some use a lot of oil to fry them, but we use very little.

Cotelettes can be made either with cooked potatoes or raw: the end result is very different. In my family we've always used cooked; however, I've grated a small piece of raw potato too, as it adds a bit more texture and taste.

Finely grate the cooked potato and raw potato into a large bowl. Add the meat, grated onion, spices, salt and pepper and knead the mixture together for about 5 minutes. Add the egg and knead for another 5 minutes. If you have the patience, continue kneading for another 5 minutes: the end result will be smoother. Or you can simply put it in a food processor fitted with a paddle and mix for less than a minute – no longer, otherwise the mixture will become doughy and stretchy as the cooked potatoes release too much starch.

Scatter the breadcrumbs evenly on a large plate or tray. Have another tray ready to hold the prepared cotelettes after you dip them in the breadcrumbs. Lastly, place some paper towels on another plate or tray for when the patties are cooked.

Take spoonfuls of the meat mixture and form into balls the size of golf balls. Roll these into logs and flatten to form a flat egg shape.

Coat each cotelette with breadcrumbs and place on the clean tray. Meanwhile, in a large frying pan on a medium heat, heat the oil until hot but not smoking. Add the cotelettes to the pan but don't overcrowd it. Fry them for about 2–3 minutes on each side; resist touching them or moving them about until they are fully cooked on each side. Turn them over one last time, give them another minute then place on paper towels and let them drain. Serve with lavash bread, sliced tomatoes and gherkins.

كوكوسبزى

KUKU SABZI
GREEN HERBED
BAKED EGGS

1 rounded tbsp butter
(optional)

4 tbsp oil

50g (2oz) 1 cup flat-leaf
parsley, finely chopped

50g (2oz) 1 cup coriander,
finely chopped

25g (1oz) ½ cup dill, finely
chopped

25g (1oz) ½ cup garlic
chives or spring onions, finely
chopped

25g (1oz) 1 cup spinach,
finely chopped

1 tbsp plain white flour
or rice flour or corn starch

1 tsp baking powder

1 tsp salt

¼ tsp pepper

7 large eggs

tiniest pinch of saffron
threads, pounded then dissolved
in 2-3 tbsp hot water (optional)

A *kuku* is similar to a Spanish *tortilla* or Italian *frittata*. Iranian *kukus* come in many different versions, from potato to meat, aubergine and walnuts, courgettes, cauliflower and spinach. Kuku Sabzi has lots and lots of chopped herbs so it becomes a vivid green colour. It is one of the main dishes gracing the Persian *Norooz* (New Year) table, as herbs are a symbol of rebirth and eggs of fertility.

The trick is not to use too much oil, to allow the freshness of the green herbs to really come through, so that it's a real spring dish. Some people add chopped lettuce instead of herbs, which makes it 'puffier'. Try adding some crushed walnuts or barberries too. Serve hot or cold, cut into wedges.

Preheat the oven to 190°C/375°F/Gas Mark 5. Place the butter, if using, and oil in an ovenproof dish and heat for 10–12 minutes. (To make small *kukus*, use silicone muffin moulds – no need to preheat.)

Place the chopped herbs and spinach in a large bowl with the flour, baking powder, salt and pepper. Beat the eggs in another bowl until just mixed and add to the herbs, along with the saffron liquid if using.

Take the dish out of the oven and pour in the egg mixture. It will bubble a bit but don't worry. Cover with a lid or some foil, put it straight back into the oven and let it cook for about 30 minutes. Uncover and allow to cook for a further 20 minutes until it is golden brown in colour.

For silicone moulds, simply fill them with the egg mixture, place in the oven and cook for about 30–35 minutes. Let them cool for a minute before inverting the *kukus* and cooling them further on a rack.

To cook on top of the stove, heat the oil and butter in a frying pan until very hot, then add the mixture. Cover, lower the heat and allow to cook for about 20–25 minutes. Put a plate over the pan and flip the *kuku* over, then slide it back into the pan and let it cook, uncovered, for a further 10–15 minutes until firm yet springy to the touch. Then flip it on to a chopping board straight away and cut into wedges.

Serve with plain cool yogurt and Sabzi Khordan (fresh herbs, page 132) or any kind of *torshi* (pickles, page 84).

The perfect picnic: individual herb *kukus* and sweet date omelettes (see page 167), plus herbs and salad

An Angel with Red Hair

The most distinct feature of Sedigh *joon* (Baba Bazargani's niece) was her bright red hair, which she set free from under her *hejab* in the middle of the town square in Ghazvin. This was in the 1920s when women were forced to wear the veil. She asked her coach driver to take her around town with her cousin who had also decided to unveil. They were driven everywhere with the wind in their hair while the men booed and threw pebbles. She was the first woman in Ghazvin to do so and she was only 16. (By the way, '*joon*' is a term of respect for older people, like the Japanese suffix '*san*'. In Persian it also means 'dear'.)

She met her second husband-to-be, Johnny, an Englishman who worked for the National Oil Company, quite late in life. She taught him Farsi and he taught her English. Once she learned the basics, she sailed to the United States in the hope of studying child education, going to school at night and cleaning people's homes by day to pay for her studies.

One day while she was cleaning, when she thought that she just couldn't do this for another day, she met Eleanor Roosevelt. She had a heartfelt conversation with her, telling her of her dreams of opening a modern orphanage in Iran. Eleanor picked up the phone and called Shahrzad Shams, the Shah's sister, who was also head of the Red Cross in Iran.

Her Royal Highness built Sedigh *joon* 12 cottages in which she could house the children she found on the streets. With help, Sedigh *joon* raised, trained and schooled 134 children. Some became professors, others became officers and one of them even dedicated a book to her called *An Angel Saved My Life*.

However, since she was doing something novel and swimming against the tide in Iran, as well as raising five children of her own, she became stressed and fell ill. She developed Lou Gehrig's disease and slowly but surely became paralysed, yet her mind was never affected. She was also the most positive person, always saying she was fine with a smile, wearing her favourite red lipstick and having her white hair dyed red, even when she could no longer move. The last time I saw her and asked how she was doing, she shook her head for the first time. She passed away a few days later. The average time a patient lives after diagnosis with Lou Gehrig's is three to five years: Sedigh *joon* lasted 36.

Now, you would think, how could this superwoman have found time to cook anything? Well she did, and one of her favourite dishes was called Kuku Ye Chekhertmeh (page 166), which she whipped up at a moment's notice. In fact, *Chekhertmeh* literally means a dish that you put together at the last minute.

FAMILY MEMOIR

Hunting and Riding

Riding was not only a pastime but a necessity in our family. Some of our land could only be reached on horseback and, as a result, my grandfather, mother, uncle, aunt and most of their cousins developed slightly bowed legs. Except for my grandmother, who rode side-saddle like the lady she was.

We often went on camping trips to some of the furthest family land. My grandfather and the boys would ride out and hunt while the women prepared the side dishes to go with the game they caught. There was fresh bread, roasted vegetables, salads, jars of *torshis* (pickles, page 84) and gherkins. The women cleaned the shot from the quails and marinated them in pomegranate molasses before barbecuing them. We sat under the stars and ate, to the sound of gas lamps and crickets, occasionally coming across a pellet or two in between bites!

My grandfather would sometimes be away for days on end since it took a long time to travel between his villages. The most important items for him were his horse and his gun – not unlike the nomadic Bakhtiari tribes. The Bakhtiaris are courageous people who roam the Iranian plateaus under harsh conditions on horseback, moving to the high mountains in the summer and to the western foothills in winter, so that their herds can eat fresh green grass. They camp wherever their sheep are grazing and cook hearty meat stews over wood fires – eating whatever is available, hunting, or killing one of the herd for food. They churn yogurt or cheese in a sheep's-stomach bag, make traditional leather goods and weave goat hair into their famous Bibibaf carpets.

My grandfather and the boys would ride out and hunt while the women prepared the side dishes to go with the game they caught

My grandfather Baba

FAMILY
MEMOIR

چخرتمه صدیق جون

KUKU YE CHEKHERTMEH

BAKED EGGS WITH CHICKEN,
NUTMEG AND CLOVES

1 medium onion, finely sliced

1 tbsp any good-quality flavourless oil

2 tbsp butter (or use extra oil instead)

2 boneless, skinless chicken breasts, cut into 2.5cm (1in) slices

⅓ tsp turmeric

1 garlic clove, finely chopped

tiny pinch of freshly grated nutmeg

pinch of ground cloves

½–1 tsp salt

few twists of pepper

4 large eggs, whisked until mixed

1 tbsp plain flour or corn starch

Sedigh *joon*'s mother Fatemeh was my grandfather's sister. When she was old, she spent most of the time in her grand brass bed in a beautiful nightdress with her white hair in two long braids. She was chubby and loved food and her children tried to put her on a diet, but she would bribe the cook Chowcat Baji to bring her treats.

One of the dishes Chowcat Baji made very well and quickly also happened to be Fatemeh's favourite – Chekhertmeh, a delicious, more-ish egg dish filled with tender shredded chicken, caramelised onions, ground cloves, nutmeg and fresh herbs. She would make this in a cast-iron pan over hot coals and when one side was ready, she would flip it up high like a crêpe to cook the other side. Later Sedigh *joon* made this for her family and her recipe was passed on to me.

Sauté the onion with the oil and butter until translucent, then add the chicken, turmeric and garlic and stir until the chicken pieces are seared but uncooked. Add the nutmeg, cloves, half the salt, pepper and stir. Spread the mixture over the bottom of the frying pan. Whisk the eggs with the remaining salt and the flour, and add to the pan.

Mix them up a little with a spatula, then reduce the heat to its lowest setting, cover and cook for about 25–30 minutes. Serve with yogurt, fresh bread and Sabzi Khordan (fresh herbs, page 132).

املت خرما

OMELETTEH KHORMA
BUTTERY SWEET DATE OMELETTE

This omelette calls for sweet dates. Date palm cultivation in Iran goes back to the time of Mesopotamia. The best dates are *Sahani* from Jahrom and *Mozafati* from the historic city of Bam – both towns are thousands of years old and are in the warm south. In fact, Jahrom means a warm place. *Sahani* are the most popular dates in Iran. *Mozafati* are the most expensive and rarely exported; they are best eaten when just ripened and juicy and so go rotten quickly. Since they are very hard to come by, you can use regular dates soaked for a few hours or steamed for 3–5 minutes. This recipe is fast and simple: serve it for breakfast or brunch. (Photograph on page 163.)

5 medium eggs

salt and pepper

pinch of turmeric

50ml (2fl oz) ¼ cup cream or milk (optional)

1 tbsp butter

8–10 dates, soaked or steamed, pitted and roughly chopped or halved

Crack the eggs in a bowl and whisk just until mixed well. Add the salt, pepper and turmeric, and cream or milk if using, and mix again.

Heat the butter in a frying pan over a medium heat until it foams but does not colour. Pour in the eggs and immediately lower the heat. Place the dates on top, cover and let it cook gently for about 5–7 minutes depending on how you like your eggs done.

Adjust the seasoning and serve with some Persian bread such as *lavash*, or plain Indian *naan*.

You can also make individual omelettes in silicone muffin moulds – follow the method on page 162.

CHAPTER SEVEN

FISH

GHALIYEH MAHI VA MEYGOO

SPICY SOUTHERN FISH STEW WITH TAMARIND

The cuisine of southern Iran is very different from the rest of the country since it is geographically close to Pakistan. Not many Iranians are familiar with it. It uses hot spices such as chillies and ginger and, being on the Persian Gulf, people eat a lot more fish than elsewhere in Iran (apart from along the Caspian coast). *Ghaliyeh* or *kalya* is an ancient term for stew.

Sour tamarind gives this dish a distinct sweet and sour flavour without using traditional lemon juice or verjuice. You can make it with either prawns or fish – reduce the cooking time to 10–12 minutes if using prawns only – but I've put them together here.

In a large frying pan sauté the onion and spring onions in the oil and butter, if using, until golden. Add the garlic and stir for another 2 minutes, making sure not to brown the onions too much. Stir in the chilli or cayenne, turmeric, ginger and curry powder. Add the herbs, salt and pepper and stir constantly for 3–5 minutes. Add the chopped tomato and stir. Mix the tamarind paste with the hot water and add to the pan. Cover and let the sauce simmer for about 20–30 minutes.

Gently slide in the fish fillets, cover and cook for about 15–20 minutes on a low heat until the fish is cooked through but not overcooked. Add the prawns and cook for another 8–10 minutes or until the fish and the prawns are fully cooked and no longer translucent. Adjust the seasoning and serve with plain rice.

TIP: You can substitute 1½ tbsp southern-style *advieh* (see page 204) for the individual spices.

1 small onion, finely sliced

4–5 spring onions, finely chopped

2 tbsp oil

1 tbsp butter (or use extra oil)

3 garlic cloves, finely chopped

½ tsp finely ground chilli powder or cayenne pepper

⅓ tsp turmeric

1 tsp chopped fresh ginger

1½ tsp mild curry powder

125g (4oz) 2 cups fresh coriander, roughly chopped

50g (2oz) 1 cup fresh fenugreek, roughly chopped or 3–4 tbsp dried

1 tsp salt

½ tsp pepper

1 large tomato, peeled, seeded and chopped

125g (4oz) ½ cup concentrated sour tamarind paste or 200g (8oz) 1 cup strained sieved tamarind pulp

900ml (1½ pints) 3½ cups hot water

500g (1lb) any firm white fish: cod, haddock or halibut

400g (13oz) raw peeled prawns

كباب ازومبرون

KABABEH OUZOMBOOROOM
LEMONY STURGEON KABAB

1kg (2lb) swordfish or monkfish, cut into roughly 8cm (3in) cubes

1 large white onion, grated

juice of 1 large lemon or juice of 1 lime plus juice of ½ orange

⅔ tsp salt

few twists of pepper

lavash or *naan* bread, to serve

lime or *narenj* (Seville orange) wedges, to serve

For the basting sauce:

juice of ½ lemon or lime

2 tbsp melted butter

½ tbsp tomato purée

The sturgeon, with its great prehistoric looks, is not only prized for its eggs but also its flesh. Meaty, tasty and oily, it is perfect for grilling and takes on a lemon and saffron marinade very well – it's more like meat than fish. This was my grandfather's favourite *kabab*. Sturgeon have been massively overfished from the Caspian sea and are now a protected species, so try this with swordfish or monkfish.

Wash the cubed fish in cold water, pat dry with paper towels and place in a bowl. Add the grated onion, lemon juice or lime and orange juices, and salt and pepper. Leave to marinate in the fridge for at least 4 hours or overnight, but no longer or the fish will 'cook' too much in the citrus juices.

Light your barbecue in advance so that it's nice and hot. Mix the ingredients for the basting sauce and set aside. Thread cubes of fish on skewers and place over the coals. Baste with the sauce a few times during the cooking, on both sides. The fish should not be overcooked: about 3–4 minutes on each side.

Check before serving: the fish should be grilled on the outside but very juicy on the inside. If it's not cooked thoroughly, grill for another minute more. Serve on top of *lavash* bread or *naan* with wedges of lime or Seville orange.

OMELETTEH ASHPAL
KUTUM ROE OMELETTE

Ashpal or fish roe is popular in Mazandaran and Gilan Provinces near the Caspian sea. People love to eat it for breakfast mashed with *kateh* (soft cooked rice, page 109) to form balls of sticky rice and roe, served with pickled garlic – not unlike a Japanese breakfast. They also mix it into other dishes, as here. Unlike other *kukus* (pages 162, 166–7), this one is slightly softer, thinner and cooks faster.

In the olden days whole fish roes were soaked in salt water and madder root in large clay jars. The jars were sealed and buried in the ground for about a year, to produce a relish or *torshi*. Roe is still salted and cured for use as a condiment.

1 very small onion
or 3 shallots, finely chopped

1 tbsp oil

½ tbsp butter

1 lobe fresh or salted *kutum*, bream, roach or cod roe

6 small eggs

⅓ tsp turmeric

salt, to taste (if using fresh roe)

pepper, to taste

1 tbsp garlic chives, chives, spring onions or dill, finely chopped (optional)

In a frying pan sauté the onion with the oil and butter until translucent and very soft. Meanwhile, clean the roe of its membranes and skin. Cut up into smaller pieces or break apart with your fingers.

Beat the eggs in a bowl and add the turmeric and roe. Pour into the pan with the onion. Use a spatula to move the egg mixture around a bit, tilting the pan so that the egg covers the bottom.

Cover the pan and let the omelette cook undisturbed for about 3 minutes on a very low heat. Flip it over if you can, otherwise let it cook for another 3 minutes with the lid on. Check the seasoning, sprinkle with the chopped herbs (although this is not traditional), and serve with fresh bread and Seer Torshi (aged pickled garlic, page 86).

Caviar in Transit

Caviar comes from the Persian word *khayedar*, short for *mahi-ye-kahyedar*, fish that bears eggs. Iranians have been catching and eating sturgeons for centuries, but were never too fond of caviar until recently. It was mainly eaten in the Caspian region as a nutritious food rather than a luxury. Once refrigerated transport became available, middle- and upper-class people in Tehran and other cities ate caviar as a delicious appetiser. Iranian children love caviar too.

There are three varieties: Beluga, Osetra and Sevruga, in order of price. Within each are three grades based on colour: Beluga ranges from light grey to black. The harder the eggs the more valuable they are. There is even a very rare golden caviar that was reserved only for the Shah, even though he was allergic to fish eggs! My grandmother's aunt Iran Lesan ol Saltaneh Ghahremani lived with the Shah's sister Ashraf. The story is that when she was brought over to the palace with her nanny to play a few times, Ashraf found her best friend and never let her go home! So she stayed and became Ashraf's closest friend and confidante until she passed away in her eighties. My grandmother Talat, who was sometimes invited to the palace with her brother Nasser Yeganeh, would come home and tell stories of the grand parties and elaborately laid tables with cut-crystal bowls of glistening golden caviar.

My own memories of caviar are mixed. When the 1979 revolution happened, it took us by complete surprise. Tehran was turned upside down. Pahlavi Street, near our home, became the scene of pitched battles between soldiers with machine guns and demonstrators burning flags. The protesters set up tents and barricades in the park where my brother and I used to play hide and seek. We watched from the house as tanks rolled by, making the ground shake and the windows rattle. At night as we lay in bed the air would be filled with sirens and gun shots. For us small kids, there was a mixture of fear and confusion tinged with real excitement.

After a few days we were forced to flee. I remember having to choose which of my toys to take. My mother hastily packed a few valuables, photographs and clothes before sweeping up my brother and me to head to the airport. None of us imagined for a second that it would be so long before we all came home and we often wondered how others who were left behind managed the many years of hardship.

Even in times of great crisis, no Iranian would dream of setting off on a journey without gifts. My mother, who by this time had remarried an American, Rodman Bundy, was determined to treat her in-laws to the finest Iranian caviar.

I remember being in transit at Heathrow, watching red-faced as melted ice dripped from the bag containing the precious fish roe. It never occurred to us that taking caviar with us might be a little crazy. We were taking something special from our country. That day will be embedded in my mind as the day my country changed for ever. We arrived in America with gifts bearing a thousand emotions.

FAMILY
MEMOIR

SABZI POLO MAHI
FRAGRANT HERBED RICE WITH FRIED FISH AND SEVILLE ORANGES

1kg (2lb) *kutum* pieces, or sole, halibut, flounder or sea bass

For the marinade (optional):
juice of ½ lemon or 1 small lime

pinch of salt and pepper

juice of ½ orange

For the herb mixture:
125g (4oz) 2 cups each of fresh parsley, coriander and dill, tough stems removed and leaves roughly chopped

25g (1oz) ½ cup spring onions (green parts) or chives or young leeks, roughly chopped

3 fresh green garlic leaves, cut into 2.5cm (1in) pieces or 2 garlic cloves, finely minced

For the rice:
600g (1lb 3oz) 3 cups rice

1½ tbsp natural yogurt

50–75g (2–3oz) ¼–⅓ cup melted butter, ghee or safflower oil, plus 1 tbsp extra

¼ tsp saffron threads, pounded

For the fish:
150g (5oz) 1 cup plain flour

½ tsp salt

pinch of pepper

oil, for frying

wedges of *narenj* (Seville oranges) or lemon, to serve

Sabzi Polo Mahi was like an anchor for my family: wherever in the world we moved to, we knew we would be eating this dish for *Norooz* or New Year's Day like almost all other Iranians. The smell of the fish frying and the herbs being steamed with the rice is an intrinsic part of the celebration for us. The fish we cooked wasn't boneless like a cod fillet, for example. It was *kutum* or Caspian roach (also known as *mahi sefid*), which has a lot of tiny sharp bones. Part of the ritual is to pick out the bones by hand before eating this dish. I did this for my husband Paul when we were dating and he says that was the moment when he knew he wanted to marry me! Any white, relatively meaty fish will do – halibut, sole or flounder – although some Russian markets sell *kutum*.

Mix together the marinade ingredients and add the fish. Leave in the fridge for about 30 minutes or up to 2 hours, but no longer or the acid from the citrus juices will 'cook' the fish. Or you can omit this step.

Mix all the chopped herbs together.

Prepare the rice by following the first steps of Polo Ba Taadig (perfect fluffy rice, page 106), up to draining and cooling. In a large saucepan, mix two ladlefuls of the rice with 75ml (3fl oz) ⅓ cup water, the yogurt, melted butter, saffron, and heat briskly. Spread over the base of the pan and layer the rice and herbs on top, shaping it into a pyramid. Finish cooking by following the method for Polo Ba Taadig.

About 15 minutes before the rice is cooked, start setting up to fry the fish. Fill a flat plate with flour (if gluten intolerant you can use gluten-free flour). Season. Pour the oil into a large non-stick frying pan to a depth of about 2.5cm (1in). Heat on a medium heat until the oil is hot but not smoking.

Dip the fish in the flour mixture on both sides then fry it. Don't crowd the pan otherwise the fish may steam instead. Place the golden fish pieces on paper towels to absorb excess oil and serve with the herbed rice and wedges of Seville oranges or lemons and Seer Torshi (aged pickled garlic, page 86).

TIP: Iranians like to eat this with smoked *kutum* (on the side of the plate, opposite), sliced, then briefly sautéed in 1 tbsp butter and 2 tbsp water, and flaked over the fried fish.

ماهی تو پر

FIFIJ (MAHI TOO POR)
POMEGRANATE-GLAZED CASPIAN FISH
STUFFED WITH HERBS AND WALNUTS

1 large male *kutum*
or Caspian roach (also known as
mahi sefid), or roach, sea bass or
red mullet

125g (4oz) 2 cups coriander,
finely chopped

3 tbsp equal amounts of
fresh mint and Asian basil,
finely chopped

1 tbsp pomegranate
molasses

1 garlic clove, very finely
chopped

1 tbsp *golpar*
(powdered hogweed seeds)

40g (1½oz) ⅓ cup walnuts,
finely crushed

few twists of pepper

1 tsp salt, plus extra to sprinkle

narenj (Seville orange) wedges
or lemon slices, to serve

The Azerbaijan Province of Iran is close to the Caspian sea. This recipe is a regional speciality and the stuffing uses plenty of fresh herbs, especially a lovely tangy green herb called *choochagh* that is only found locally, growing near streams. The best substitute I've found is a mix of equal quantities of finely chopped fresh mint and Asian basil. Use a whole fish and stuff the cavity, roll the stuffing up inside fish fillets or sandwich it between two fillets.

Traditionally, the dish is cooked in a clay pot or *gamej*, similar to a Moroccan tagine; the fish rests on a bed of thin wooden sticks and cooks very slowly for 4–5 hours. There are several different variations and this one was kindly given to me by Mrs Simine Varasteh, the mother of one of my closest friends, whose family is from the region – she used to eat this dish as a child.

Preheat the oven to 180°C/350°F/Gas Mark 4. Clean the fish and dry it completely. Place all the rest of the ingredients, except for ½ tsp salt and the orange wedges, in a large bowl and mix well. Spoon the mixture into the fish's cavity. Close it shut with a kitchen-friendly needle and thread, or use metal or soaked wooden skewers. Rub the fish with the rest of the salt and sprinkle a bit on top. Cover with foil. Cook for about 35 minutes or so, until the flesh is opaque.

Serve with *narenj* (Seville orange) wedges or lemon slices along with rice (*polo*, page 106 or *kateh*, page 109).

TIP: If you can find a tub of thick pomegranate paste, it's even better than molasses – it's more concentrated in flavour. The stuffing needs to be more sour than sweet.

MEYGOO POLO
SPICED RICE WITH PLUMP PRAWNS
AND FRESH HERBS

The spicier cuisine of the very southern part of Iran is distinctly different from the rest of the country. In the *Unani* doctrine of hot and cold foods (page 16), spicier foods are best eaten in hot and humid areas. And so spicing is heavier in the south and sometimes even a little chilli is used – considered a sacrilege elsewhere, as fresh unmasked ingredients are prized.

Iran's Gulf shrimps and prawns are plump and tasty. This recipe is Iran's answer to shrimp fried rice but with lots of spices and the addition of distinctly Persian herbs such as fresh fenugreek and coriander. Any prawns (fresh or frozen) will do, but if you have guests try tiger prawns.

Marinate the prawns in the lemon juice, coriander, chopped garlic, fresh ginger, turmeric, half of the saffron liquid, olive oil or ghee and salt and pepper. Rub the marinade gently into the prawns and let them marinate in the fridge for about 30 minutes or up to 2 hours, but no longer, or the prawns may partially 'cook' in the lemon juice.

Prepare the rice by following the first steps of Polo Ba Taadig (perfect fluffy rice, page 106), up to draining and cooling.

In a large saucepan, sauté the onion in the oil or ghee until light gold. Add the marinated prawns and cook for only a minute on both sides just so that they take on some colour but remain raw on the inside. Add the chopped coriander, bay leaves, southern spice mix, fenugreek and salt and toss for a minute in the pan. Remove from the heat and set aside. Check the seasoning and remove the bay leaves.

In a large pan, mix two ladlefuls of the rice with the yogurt, melted butter, remaining saffron liquid and 75ml (3fl oz) ⅓ cup water. Heat briskly then spread over the base of the pan. Layer the rice with the prawn mixture on top, shaping it into a pyramid. Finish cooking following the method for Polo Ba Taadig.

625g (1¼lb) prawns, shelled and de-veined

For the marinade:

juice of 1 small lemon

1 tbsp fresh coriander, finely chopped

3 garlic cloves, finely chopped

1 tsp fresh ginger, grated

¼ tsp turmeric

⅓ tsp saffron threads, pounded then dissolved in 2–3 tbsp hot water

1 tbsp olive oil or ghee

salt and pepper

For the rice:

600g (1lb 3oz) 3 cups rice

1½ tbsp natural yogurt

50–75g (2–3oz) ¼–⅓ cup melted butter, ghee or safflower oil, plus 1 tbsp extra

For the prawn mixture:

1 large onion, thinly sliced

250ml (8fl oz) 1 cup oil or ghee

150g (5oz) ¾ cup fresh coriander, finely chopped

2 bay leaves

2 tbsp *advieh* southern spice mix (see page 204)

15g (½oz) ⅓ cup fresh fenugreek, finely chopped

1 tsp salt

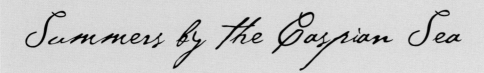

Summers by the Caspian Sea

My maternal grandparents had the most perfect house by the Caspian sea. After losing practically everything in the Shah's White Revolution in the 1960s, they moved to a small town called Shahsavar. They bought a pastel-coloured villa in the middle of a beautiful garden filled with oranges, lemons, mandarins, *narenj* (Seville oranges) and kumquats. The house was elevated, with a long wide staircase leading up to it and a large terrace all around it. The furniture was Russian wood – simple and summery – and the house was dotted with heirloom carpets and *gilims*.

Grandfather loved to sit on the terrace at dusk. My grandmother Talat laid the table outside with his favourite light supper of dried village bread and Mast o Khiar (cold cucumber soup, page 136). He would always raise his glass and say '*za vashe zdorovie!*' or 'cheers!' in Russian, as his family was from Leningrad and Baku.

Just a few metres away from the sea, the moist salty air would fill the house, mingling with the orange blossoms to create an everlasting memory in all of us. The sea air on the coast of California – or anywhere else that reminds us of the Caspian – instantly takes us back to those summer days.

We loved that house. The most important thing to us as children was that we were free to do as we wished. There was no longer a living room that only guests were allowed to enter, or something antique that we weren't allowed to touch. Everything was there to be touched, explored and jumped on!

Outside, we climbed the trees and picked any fruit we liked. We went out on our bicycles until dark, swam in the shallow Caspian sea and ran back home covered in sand, and no one told us off, but rather gave us a pat on the head or a kiss on the cheek. There were always people coming and going and friends ringing the doorbell to come and play. We would bring stray puppies home and give them baths and names and they would chew the couch and pee everywhere. We took long naps and woke up to tea and freshly baked yogurt cake, or slept under the stars in the garden, dragging out beds and mosquito nets.

Everything in the Caspian was magnified. Because of the high moisture in the air, smells were stronger, appetites bigger and sleep much deeper.

> Just a few metres away from the sea, the moist salty air would fill the house, mingling with the orange blossoms to create an everlasting memory in all of us

FAMILY
MEMOIR

کیاهان

CHAPTER EIGHT

HERBS

باقالی قاتق

BAGHALI GHATOGH

FRESH BROAD BEANS WITH DILL,
GARLIC AND POACHED EGGS

125g (4oz) 1 cup fresh broad beans, shelled and skinned (see Tip, below)

50g (2oz) butter

2 tbsp olive oil

6–7 garlic cloves, finely chopped

125g (4oz) 2 cups fresh dill, roughly chopped

1 tsp turmeric

500ml (17fl oz) 2 cups hot water

salt

3–4 eggs

This is a quintessential Caspian dish with garlic, fresh dill, fresh beans and eggs. The recipe is quick to prepare and takes me straight back to the region with its warm salty climate. The most important thing is to use fresh ingredients. Although you can create a tasty version with frozen beans, try to use fresh dill.

Sauté all the ingredients – apart from the water, salt and eggs – together in a large frying pan for about 15 minutes on a medium heat.

Add the hot water and let the mixture simmer for about 15 minutes. Do not allow it to boil hard, otherwise the beans may fall apart. Check occasionally and if the mixture looks too dry add up to 125ml (4fl oz) ½ cup more hot water.

By now the oil will have risen to the top. Add the salt, then break the eggs over the bean mixture, cover the pan and let the eggs cook until they are done but ever so slightly runny in the middle. Serve with bread or a lovely hot steaming bowl of Polo Ba Taadig (perfect fluffy rice, page 106) and Seer Torshi (aged pickled garlic, page 86).

TIP: This recipe is traditionally made with *baghali sefid* – beans that look like white peanuts. You may find them on sale in Middle Eastern shops, but broad beans are fine. To skin broad beans, place them in a bowl and pour boiling water over them. Leave for a couple of minutes, then drain in a colander and run under the cold tap. The skins should come off easily using your fingers.

قرمه سبزی

GHORMEH SABZI
FOUR-HERB STEW
WITH TENDER MEAT

1 large onion, finely chopped

500g (1lb) stewing beef or
de-boned leg of lamb,
cut into 8-10cm (3-4in) cubes

3 tbsp any good-quality
flavourless oil

1-2 garlic cloves

1 tsp turmeric

few twists of pepper

750ml (1¼ pints) 3 cups hot
water

100g (3½oz) 1 cup red
kidney beans, soaked
overnight or for at least 6 hours

25g (1oz) ½ cup fresh
fenugreek, finely chopped

50g (2oz) 1 cup coriander,
finely chopped

75g (3oz) 1½ cups garlic
chives, finely chopped

125g (4oz) 2 cups curly or
flat-leaf parsley, finely chopped

5 Omani limes, pierced several
times with the tip of a knife

½-1 tsp salt

juice of ½ lemon

Non-Iranians either love this dish or hate it. I hope you'll be a convert. The deep green stew is dotted with red beans, Omani limes and chunks of tender beef that fall apart on the fork. It's lemony, fresh with herbs and deeply rich in all its greenness.

Don't eat Ghormeh Sabzi before a date or an important meeting. Generally Persian food doesn't have a strong odour that will make you or your home smell. But Ghormeh Sabzi is the exception that breaks the rule. My grandmother often skipped the *shambalileh* (fenugreek) since it is the main culprit. You can do the same, but it is a shame as it gives the dish a distinct flavour. Substitute firm tofu for the beef and Ghormeh Sabzi becomes an excellent vegetarian meal.

In a large saucepan, sauté the onion and meat in 2 tbsp oil, then add the garlic. Stir, add the turmeric and pepper, then the hot water. Let it boil on high for about 3–4 minutes, skimming the top. Add the drained beans, bring back to the boil, and boil for 10 minutes. Lower the heat and cook for about 45 minutes, skimming if you need to.

While the meat is cooking, in a non-stick frying pan sauté all of the chopped herbs in the remaining oil over a medium-low heat, stirring continuously, making sure they don't catch at the bottom and burn. This will take about 10 minutes – some people like to fry them for at least 20–25 minutes but your stew will be less 'fresh' if you do. You'll know when it's ready when the smell of the herbs fills the air.

Add the herbs to the meat with the Omani limes and the salt and cook for another 20–30 minutes or until the meat is super-tender. Check the seasoning and add the lemon juice if necessary. Serve with plain rice and Sabzi Khordan (fresh herbs, page 132).

TIP: Persian food shops often sell fresh or frozen mixed herbs for this *khoresht* (stew), so if you do come across them, stock up – it will cut the preparation substantially. You can buy pre-sautéed herbs to make it easier, as the stirring stage of the herbs is what puts people off making it, but it is so worth it!

ترشی لیته

TORSHIYEH LITEH
PICKLED AUBERGINES WITH TARRAGON, NIGELLA SEEDS AND FRESH HERBS

1½kg (3lb) aubergines, skin left on

1 litre (1¾ pints) 4 cups white wine vinegar, white grape vinegar or white vinegar

1 large onion, roughly chopped

5 garlic cloves, roughly chopped

400g (13oz) 8 cups mixed fresh herbs, including mint, coriander or flat-leaf parsley, and tarragon, roughly chopped

½ tsp nigella seeds

½ tsp whole coriander seeds

3 tsp salt

½ tsp black pepper

In Iran, we pickle everything – from the usual to the unusual, including dates, watermelon, grapes, sour cherries and persimmons – to serve with stews, rice dishes and *kababs*. *Torshi* (pickle) comes from the Persian *torsh* or sour. They are generally salty, sometimes sweet and sour, flavoured with herbs or seeds – but never spicy (with the exception of southern-style *torshi*, though even that is mild in comparison to Indian pickles).

This is a great pickle with lots of layers of flavour. The meatiness of the aubergine complements the vinegar, nigella seeds and tarragon, while its lovely crunch goes particularly well with *kababs* and other meaty dishes, cutting through the richness.

Preheat the oven to 180°C/350°F/Gas Mark 4. Cut the aubergines into 5cm (2in) cubes and put them on a tray in the oven for about 20–30 minutes to remove the moisture and soften them a bit. Leave to cool then tip them into a stainless-steel saucepan, cover with some of the vinegar and boil for a minute or two.

Meanwhile, put the rest of the vinegar and all of the other ingredients in a big bowl. Add the semi-cooked aubergine mixture and toss together. Put the mixture in a food processor and whizz a couple of times to get a chunky consistency. (Or, instead of using a food processor, simply chop all the ingredients finely before you start.)

Pot in sterilised jars and leave in a cool dark place for about a month before eating.

خیار شور

KHIAR SHOOR
CRUNCHY PICKLED CUCUMBERS OR
GHERKINS WITH TARRAGON

2kg (4lb) small pickling
cucumbers, 13–15cm (5–6in)
long, if possible with stalks
in place

sprigs of tarragon

whole garlic cloves,
peeled

whole peppercorns

2 litres (3½ pints) 7 cups
white wine vinegar or white
grape vinegar

7–8 tbsp salt

Iranians like their pickles to be super-crunchy and vinegary with only a hint of sweetness. My grandmother Talat was famous for her Khiar Shoor. In fact, when she passed away, after the mourning was over, there was a lot of debate as to who should get the last jar left in the pantry. Her only son was the lucky recipient.

Persian cucumbers are famous for being compact, crunchy and full of flavour, which is what you'll need to bear in mind when buying cucumbers to make this pickle. Look for them in Middle Eastern shops.

The recipe is effortless. Follow the quantities if your family are big fans of pickle or if you want enough to last you for a while. Otherwise, halve them.

Sterilise a selection of jars. Wash the cucumbers. Leave the stalks on as they will help keep the extra moisture out and make them super-crunchy. Wash the tarragon and make sure the sprigs are dry.

Pack the cucumbers into the jars, side by side, adding as many as possible but leaving room for the vinegar. Tuck a sprig of tarragon, 2 garlic cloves and 2–3 peppercorns into each jar.

In a jug, mix the vinegar with the salt, then fill the jars. Seal and store in a cool dark dry place for a minimum of 10 weeks before consuming.

Town and Country

My grandmother Talat was a city girl but my grandfather was country all the way. She loved parties, playing her violin and dressing in Dior, while he loved to ride his horses or get his hands dirty digging radishes. Their lives were divided between Tehran and villages near the town of Ghazvin, where they would spend the summer with their children and some 40 or so cousins.

In Tehran, my grandmother would close off the living room to everyone but guests, hide the fancy sweets from the children in cherry-wood cupboards and have her silver and crystal polished regularly. Her friends ranged from politicians to writers to musicians; they gathered round to play the piano or *setar* (lute), drink, laugh and be social butterflies. The children had piano lessons, went to parties, not to mention the annual festivities, weddings, funerals and family visits. There was always something to do or a function to attend.

In the country, it was a different story. Time slowed down. Adults came to relax and enjoy a bowl of Mast o Khiar (cold cucumber soup, page 136) under a tree. They read poetry, enjoyed the early evening light, or listened to the sound of running water from a nearby stream.

My grandmother let her hair down. She wore flowery dresses and helped prepare food for all the visitors. The Bazarganis' house was the most popular with the kids because they could do as they pleased. There was a feast every day: stuffed roast turkey, whole lamb or different juicy *kababs*, fruity rice dishes, *mazzes* (appetisers) such as *boorani* (vegetables and yogurt, pages 94, 100), salads, barbecued corn on the cob and sweet beetroots, all fresh from the farm. Children would help pick cucumbers and tomatoes for lunch or milk a cow to make rice pudding. At dusk they watched the ducks, geese, dogs and chickens all gather to feed.

My grandparents were loved and respected by the villagers. So much so that hundreds would turn out to celebrate my mother's birthday. The villagers followed what they did and heard news of them via servants working in the city. They were almost like celebrities to them! Everyone's lives were intertwined through the land.

In the country, it was a different story. Time slowed down. Adults came to relax and enjoy a bowl of Mast o Khiar under a tree. They read poetry, enjoyed the early evening light, or listened to the sound of running water from a nearby stream

سکنجبین

SEKANJEBEEN
SWEET SHARP MINT AND
VINEGAR SYRUP

675g (1lb 6oz) 3 cups caster
sugar

600ml (1 pint) 2⅔ cups
white wine vinegar
or white grape vinegar

about 50 fresh mint leaves

This delicate clear thick syrup is pure sweetness and
fresh mint. Sharhzad Dowlatshahi, who was married to my
mother's cousin, Behzad Mohit, gave me the recipe. She
used to tie her beautiful Andie MacDowell-style hair up
and set the table with bottles waiting to be filled, while
the syrup bubbled away on the stove. Her whole house
smelled heavenly for days.

You can dilute it like a cordial to drink, and she also
served it in summer for dipping lettuce leaves in. The
contrast between the cool lettuce hearts and the thick
liquid is fabulous – it makes a good party dish. Her
daughters and I would sit with a tray in front of us in the
shaded garden, dipping and chatting away about food.
They eventually became serious foodies, opening a series
of popular trendy restaurants around northern Tehran
serving Asian, French and Californian dishes.

Boil the sugar with 2 litres (3½ pints) 8 cups of water in a saucepan.
Let it bubble away for about 10 minutes over a medium heat, making
sure to stir it once in a while.

Add the vinegar and boil for another 10–15 minutes until the liquid
thickens and a syrup forms. Add the mint leaves and boil for another
2 minutes. Remove from the heat and cool before straining and
bottling in sterilised bottles. Store in a cool dark place.

TIP: Try grating a small unpeeled cucumber in each glass before
adding the syrup, water and ice cubes for a refreshing summer drink.

KHORESHTEH RIVAS

PINK RHUBARB
AND MINT STEW

1 large onion

1 celery stalk (optional)

500g (1lb) de-boned leg
of lamb or stewing beef, cut into
4–5cm (1½–2in) cubes or 1kg (2lb)
chicken breast pieces on the bone

2 tbsp olive oil

2 garlic cloves

2 tbsp butter

½ tsp turmeric

1 tsp brown sugar

juice and zest of ½ lemon

1–1½ tsp salt

½ tsp white pepper

25g (1oz) ½ cup fresh mint,
finely chopped

150g (5oz) 3 cups flat-leaf
parsley, roughly chopped

750ml (17fl oz) 3 cups
unsalted chicken stock
or hot water

⅓ tsp dried mint

750g (1½lb) rhubarb, cut
diagonally into 5cm (2in) pieces

½ tsp saffron threads,
pounded then dissolved in
2–3 tbsp hot water

Rhubarb is native to Iran and has been grown for
thousands of years. In Zoroastrian mythology, Mashye
and Mashyane, the first mortal human couple (not unlike
Adam and Eve), arose from mother earth in the form of a
rhubarb plant. This *khoresht* (stew) is very much in line
with the typical Persian way of balancing sweet and sour
flavourings in their dishes. Some people omit the herbs
altogether from this dish, making it a deep golden yellow.
However, I think mint and rhubarb create a memorable
combination.

When rhubarb is not in season, use celery and adjust
the taste with some sugar and lemon juice and you have
another dish called Khoreshteh Karafss.

Chop the onion and celery into small cubes or mirepoix. In a heavy
frying pan over a medium-high heat, brown the mirepoix and the meat
in the olive oil until the vegetables are golden and the meat is seared –
about 10 minutes. Stirring frequently, add the garlic, butter, turmeric,
sugar, lemon zest and salt and pepper. Stir in the fresh herbs. Cook
for about 5 minutes. Add the stock or water and the dried mint.

Cover and simmer on the lowest setting for about an hour. Check
and gently stir the stew 2–3 times during the cooking process.

Add the rhubarb, lemon juice and saffron liquid, cover again and
let it cook for another 20–30 minutes – without stirring too much this
time to avoid breaking up the rhubarb.

Check the seasoning: if it's too tart, add more sugar and if not tart
enough, balance it out with a little more lemon juice.

TIP: For chicken reduce the cooking time to 20 minutes for the first
stage, then add the rhubarb and cook for a further 30 minutes until the
meat is tender. Omit the meat altogether for a vegetarian dish.
A useful tip when making any stew is to leave the lid slightly ajar while
it's simmering, to allow some of the steam to escape.

BAGHALI POLO BA MAHICHEH
DILLED RICE WITH FRESH BROAD BEANS AND TENDER SPRING LAMB

Baghali Polo is the king of layered rice dishes. It contains lots of chopped green fragrant dill and steaming rice, hiding pieces of hot slow-cooked melt-in-the-mouth lamb shank and vibrant tender broad beans. It captures the beginning of spring perfectly as the recipe makes sure everything retains its colour and fragrance. But there's no need to wait until spring to make this dish. It can be easily prepared by using frozen dill and broad beans at any time of year.

Sauté the lamb and onion together in the oil on a high heat until sizzling and no liquid remains – about 8–10 minutes. This method ensures that the onion flavour goes deep into the meat, so that the meaty smell disappears.

Add the tomato purée and stir. Add the turmeric and fry until the meat is no longer red. Season. Pour in the boiling water, cover, and lower the heat. Simmer the lamb for 2½ hours, stirring occasionally, until the meat is super-tender.

Prepare the rice by following the first steps of Polo Ba Taadig (perfect fluffy rice, page 106), until the rice is *al dente*, but adding 1 tbsp of the dill to the water you cook the rice in. This little trick will make the rice turn a pretty light green. Add the shelled broad beans right at the very end before draining the rice. Once the rice is *al dente*, remove from heat and drain and cool.

In the same pan, put the melted butter, 75ml (3fl oz) ⅓ cup water, the yogurt, saffron and 2 ladlefuls of the rice. Mix and heat through on a medium-high heat. Spread the mixture over the base of the pan. Start layering the broad beans and rice mixture with the fresh dill, shaping it like a pyramid as you go. Finish cooking the rice following the method for Polo Ba Taadig.

Once everything is cooked, you can either layer the rice with the lamb in a serving dish and serve the sauce on the side or serve the meat in its juices in a separate dish. Serve with either yogurt or *torshi* (pickles, page 86).

750g (1½lb) lamb shanks

1 large onion, diced

3–4 tbsp olive oil

1 tsp tomato purée

½ tsp turmeric

salt and pepper

1.2 litres (2 pints) 5 cups boiling water

For the rice:

600g (1lb 3oz) 3 cups rice

75g (3oz) 1½ cups chopped fresh or frozen dill

200g (7oz) 1½ cups broad beans, fresh or frozen, shelled

50–75g (2–3oz) ¼–⅓ cup melted butter, ghee or safflower oil, plus 1 tbsp extra

1½ tbsp natural yogurt

⅓ tsp saffron threads, pounded

New Year Celebration

Persian New Year, or *Norooz*, is the most celebrated and festive day in Iran and the holiest day in the Zoroastrian religion. *Norooz* literally means 'new day' and it falls on the spring equinox around 20 or 21 March, marking the official start of spring.

There is a lot of excitement in Iranian households come *Norooz*. It's just like Christmas when you know you'll be getting presents, eating delicious food, and everyone is in a good mood. The radio is on and there's lots of hustle and bustle. Everything needs to be clean and shiny, and people must wear at least one new item of clothing.

My grandfather and his brothers played backgammon or chess, the women were busy frying fish and steaming dilled rice, while we children were running around. We grabbed at food – it was the only day we were allowed to eat what we wanted just because our parents were simply too busy to monitor us.

In every Iranian home the *Haftseen* is the centrepiece of *Norooz* celebrations. The *Haftseen*, literally seven *seens* – things that begin with the letter S – is a special table laid with symbolic items such as *seeb* (apples), *sekkeh* (coins) and *sabzeh* (wheat, barley or lentil sprouts growing in a dish).

Strangely for a ritual with pagan roots, the *Haftseen* also usually holds a book – generally the Koran or a book by one of the great Persian poets such as Hafez or Ferdowsi. Following the Arab conquests that brought Islam to Iran, placing the Koran on the *Haftseen* somehow legitimised or validated the custom from an Islamic viewpoint and allowed it to continue – a perfect example of Persian adaptability (while maintaining a remarkably enduring core culture).

Later, as parts of society became more secular, some people replaced the Koran with books that they felt better represented their sense of spirituality, like the *Divan* of Hafez, or the *Shahnameh* by Ferdowsi. At home, we set out a copy of Hafez's poetry, which, as is Persian tradition, would be picked up and opened on a random page and the verses we read were said to foretell our future for the coming year.

Lastly and most importantly, everyone gathers around the *Haftseen* as the clock strikes the first hour of the year, which varies from year to year according to the lunar calendar. They say that whatever mood you are in at *Norooz* you will be that way for the rest of the year, so people make sure they are on their best behaviour.

Two other important festivities form part of the celebrations. *Chaharshanbeh suri*, literally Red Wednesday or the Festival of Fire, takes place on the eve of the last Wednesday of the year. People light bonfires in their gardens or even on the pavement outside their homes and jump over them singing '*zardi-ye man az to, sorkhi-ye to az man*', meaning 'give me your fiery glow and take away my sickly pallor'. It's another hugely popular festival with children, who get to stay out late, play with sparklers, watch firework displays and go trick or treating.

FAMILY
MEMOIR

ادویجات

CHAPTER NINE

SPICES

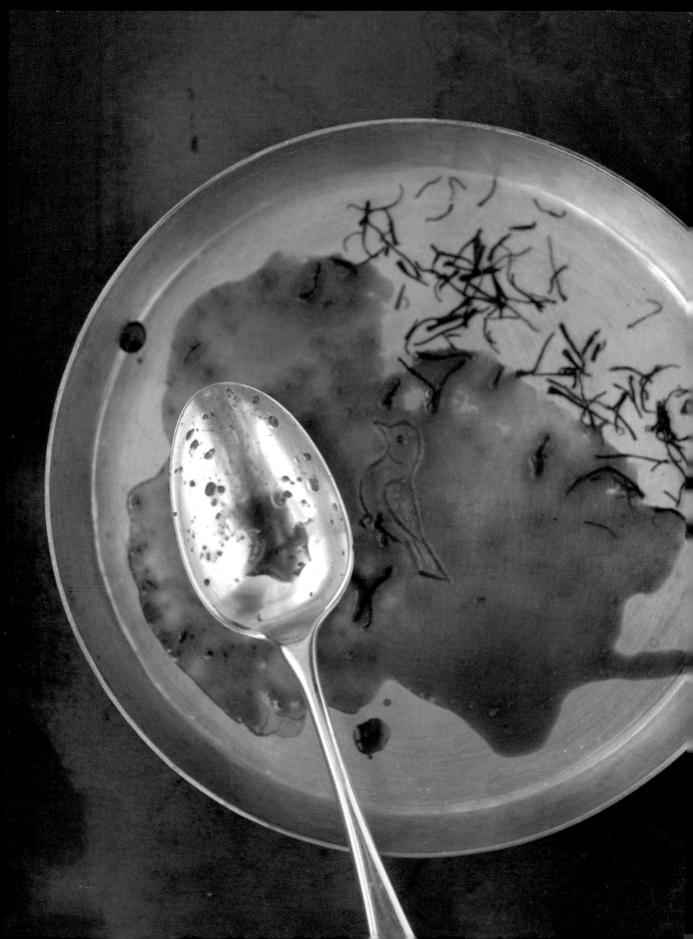

بستنی اکبر مشتی

BASTANIYEH AKBAR MASHTI
WILD ORCHID ICE CREAM

Akbar Mashti was an enterprising young man who created this recipe back in the 1920s. It's a blend of crunchy pistachios, heady rose water and fragrant saffron. The texture is stretchier than regular ice cream, because the powdered root of a wild orchid (*Orchis mascula*) or salep is used in the custard. Salep is sold in packets in Middle Eastern shops.

In Iran, the ice cream is scooped in between two delicate, almost transparent, rice wafers – like a sandwich. As a child, I remember biting into these cold fragrant discs, eagerly searching for pieces of pistachio and chunks of frozen cream. That's why I've made sure you'll find an extra helping of them in my recipe.

250ml (8fl oz) 1 cup whole milk

125g (4oz) ½ cup sugar

6 small organic egg yolks

2 tsp salep powder

tiny pinch of saffron threads, pounded then dissolved in 1 tbsp hot water

½ tsp rose water

250g (8oz) 1 cup double cream

3 tbsp icing sugar

3 tbsp slivered pistachios

Place the milk and 1 tsp of the sugar in a saucepan and heat, but try not to let it come to the boil. The sugar will stop the milk from boiling over. Remove from the heat and cool slightly.

Prepare a medium bowl and fine-meshed sieve for the finished crème anglaise, along with a large bowl filled with ice.

Whisk the yolks and rest of the sugar until just mixed then pour the hot milk on them in three stages, so that the eggs can get used to the heat and won't curdle.

Pour the mixture back into the pan. Place over a medium-low heat and stir continuously with a wooden spoon until pale and creamy – about 4–5 minutes. Don't allow it to come to the boil or the mixture will curdle. Once you see a lot of steam rising, around 82°C/180°F if you're using a thermometer, take the pan off the heat. Or take the spoon out of the pan and draw your finger over the back of it: if it leaves an impression that does not run, the custard is ready.

Add the salep powder, saffron liquid and rose water and whisk vigorously for a few seconds so that there are no lumps and the mixture takes on a lovely saffron hue. Remove from the heat.

Strain the custard through the sieve and into the bowl you have ready. Stand the bowl of custard over the ice bath and stir occasionally until it has cooled. Mix the double cream with the icing sugar. Pour into a 20cm (8in) tray or container and freeze it.

Pour the custard into an ice-cream maker. While it's running, break the frozen cream into 1cm (½in) chunks. Once the custard is frozen, fold in the chunks and the slivered pistachios, then freeze for a couple of hours before serving.

SHOLEH ZARD
TRADITIONAL SAFFRON RICE PUDDING
WITH PISTACHIOS

200g (7oz) 1 cup basmati
rice

875g (1¾lb) 4 cups sugar

2 rounded tbsp butter

⅓ tsp saffron threads,
pounded then dissolved in
2–3 tbsp hot water

75–125ml (3–4fl oz) ⅓–½
cup rose water

slivered almonds and
pistachios, to serve

cinnamon powder, to serve

My grandmother Talat used to make this pudding for us as kids and I loved eating it cold, straight from the fridge. The name literally means yellow (*zard*) fire (*sholeh*). To me they were like bowls of sunshine with so much saffron you didn't know what had hit you. She made pretty designs with powdered cinnamon on them, and placed slivers of bright green pistachios in the shape of flowers. It was only later that I understood the significance of *Sholeh Zard* when they were served at funerals, weddings and for the feast of *Nazri* where food is distributed to the poor. The puddings symbolise the pledge you are making.

Every household has their own version, adjusting the sweetness to their preferred taste. You can use arborio rice, which is similar to the Iranian rice *gherdeh* (which means fat, as in fat grains), but traditionally this recipe is made with basmati rice. This is our family recipe.

Place the rice in a bowl and wash it, discarding the water. Repeat 2–3 times until the water runs clear, which means the extra starch has been removed. Put the rice in a heavy saucepan with around 3 litres (5 pints) 12 cups of water and cook on high until the water starts to boil. Skim off any rising foam, stir, then lower the heat and cover. Let the rice simmer slowly for about an hour, stirring occasionally so that it doesn't stick to the bottom of the pan. Stir it gently and do not overstir or the rice will become mushy.

Add the sugar, butter and saffron liquid, and cook for another 20 minutes. By then the rice should be soft and tender with barely any liquid left – if not, cook for a little longer. When the surface becomes creamy or *La Ab Endakhteh*, it's a sign that the rice pudding is ready.

Add the rose water just before taking it off the heat. Pour into one large bowl or individual bowls. Cool then chill them in the fridge. Serve with slivers of almonds and pistachios as well as cinnamon powder.

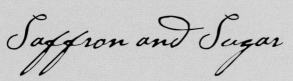

Saffron and Sugar

When we went on holiday, my mother always took a box of saffron and a tiny pocket-size pestle and mortar. She would instantly create Persian feasts from local produce and delight guests with it, jazzing up ordinary dishes such as eggs, rice, chicken, soup and rice pudding. Like a Persian fairy princess she would sprinkle food with the red-orange stems and make everything turn to gold!

Saffron is one of Iran's most famous exports. It grows mainly in the dry Khorasan region in eastern Iran. Its name comes from the Persian word *zafaran*, which in turn comes from *zarparan* or yellow leaves. The plants are members of the crocus family and the flower is a beautiful mauve with three bright orange tendrils (technically stigmas) protruding from it. These tendrils, hand-picked in one of the most painstaking harvests imaginable, are dried and used in cooking, medicine and for dyeing fabric. The difficulty of harvesting is one of the reasons why saffron is by far the most expensive spice, pound-for-pound. One pound contains tens of thousands of tendrils, more commonly referred to as 'threads'.

Iranian saffron is categorised into three different grades. *Sargol* or *Sar Ghalam*, the best, being bright deep red; *Pushali*, a slightly lighter colour; and *Dasteh* or *Dokhtar Pich*, which is both the red tip and the less valuable pale 'stem'. It is best stored in the freezer. To allow the full aroma and flavour to come through, saffron needs to be ground in a pestle and mortar before adding a few tablespoons of hot water. Then it is ready to be used in cooking.

Saffron is often used to tint *nabat*, rock sugar crystals for sweetening teas, also used as a medicinal remedy (see *Unani*, page 16). Each sugar crystal façade is like a matte transparent mirror or an uncut diamond, capturing and reflecting the light. Stacked on top of one another in the bazaar they can be mistaken for jewellery. They remind me of my Auntie Monir's highly acclaimed geometric glass work. Monir Shahroudy Farmanfarmaian is my mother's first cousin. Her fascinating life story is told in her autobiography *A Mirror Garden*, which takes the reader from her childhood playing among the orchards in Ghazvin, all the way to the USA, where she worked alongside Andy Warhol, later becoming an international artist in her own right. Now in her eighties, her work is displayed in New York's Metropolitan Museum and the V&A in London. Her *Aineh Kari* (mirror work) was initially inspired by a mirrored shrine in Shiraz where she watched the images of crowds of people reflected on the walls and ceilings.

Like a Persian fairy princess she would sprinkle food with the red-orange stems and make everything turn to gold!

BAGHLAVA
PERSIAN BAKLAVA

1 packet store-bought all-butter pâte brisée or shortcrust, pie or tart dough (all unsweetened) or use filo pastry, although it's not traditional

For the syrup:

400g (13oz) 2 cups caster sugar

125ml (4fl oz) ½ cup rose water

For the topping and for oiling:

75ml (3fl oz) ⅓ cup melted butter, ghee or oil

For the filling:

600g (1lb 3½oz) 7 cups ground blanched almonds or raw ground pistachios or 1:1 ratio of both, plus slivers of pistachio to decorate

2 tbsp ground cardamom

400g (13oz) 2 cups caster sugar

This is Persian *baghlava*, which is simply two thin layers of dough filled with saffron, pistachios or almonds, with rose-petal syrup poured over. It is very different from the elaborate *baklava* of the rest of the Middle East, but when you bite into one, you'll be hooked.

My grandmother's sister Eshrat was renowned in the family for her *baghlava*. I once baked some with her and thought I'd go crazy, as she didn't have any measuring cups and her rolling pin was so long that it knocked over everything in sight. But when the *baghlava* was baked to perfection and she poured the rose syrup on it while it was still piping hot, I knew that my hair-pulling session was worth it. Here is her recipe.

Make the syrup by boiling the sugar with 375ml (13fl oz) 1½ cups water for about 10 minutes. Add the rose water and let it cool. Brush the base and sides of a shallow metal tray with some melted butter or oil.

Prepare the filling by putting the nuts, cardamom and sugar in a food processor. Whizz until you get a fine sand-like crumb.

Preheat the oven to 150°C/350°F/Gas Mark 4.

Lightly flour a work surface and roll out half of the dough as thinly as possible. It needs to be larger than the tray. Use a rolling pin to lift the dough and place it on the tray, letting the sides hang over. Spread the nut mixture over the dough. Press it down to make it compact.

Roll out the second piece of dough, again as thinly as possible, and place on top, gently pressing down. Pinch the sides of the dough, gathering it in an upward motion to seal the *baghlava*. With a small sharp knife draw around the edge of the tray. Then draw a diagonal line from one corner to the opposite corner, and continue to add parallel lines. Repeat in the other direction.

Brush the top evenly with the remaining butter or oil. Bake for 25–30 minutes, turning the tray halfway through. The *baghlava* should be light golden bronze. Pour the syrup over the hot *baghlava* then top the diamonds with a few slivers of pistachio. Resist eating it right away! The *baghlava* needs to 'sit' for at least 8 hours. I promise it's worth the wait.

Sweet tooth: cardamom-scented Persian *baghlava*, plus *gaz* (nougat, *top left*) and *nabat* (rock sugar candy, *top right*)

ADVIEH
MY PERSIAN SPICE MIX

Advieh is the Persian version of Chinese five-spice, Moroccan *ras-el-hanout* and Indian *garam masaleh*, which incidentally originated in Iran before the moguls took it to India (in Farsi, *garm* means warm and *masaleh* an object). But unlike its Indian counterpart, which is stronger and more vibrant in flavour, *advieh* doesn't contain chillies and is generally more subtle and delicate, blended from dried roses, lime powder, cinnamon, turmeric and saffron.

There are several types of *advieh* in Persian cuisine: one for *khoresht* (stews) and one used for *polos* (rice dishes). *Advieh* is a word on loan from Arabic, meaning medicine. In fact, in the *Unani* doctrine (page 16), many spices are used not only for their flavour but also for their health benefits. Turmeric is used in meat dishes for masking the strong smell of meat and it also has astringent qualities.

In the north and north-west, where Iran borders Russia and Turkey, spices are delicate and subtle, with more cinnamon and saffron being used. At the opposite extreme in the south, ginger, chilli, coriander and cumin reflect the influence of Arab and Pakistani neighbours – though some Iranians still say no to chilli.

In the olden days, my grandmother used to order her spices from the bazaar, and she asked them to make her a special blend too. As always, it's best to buy and mix your spices a little at a time to ensure freshness. I've come up with a range of spice mixes of my own, which I've matched to the colour of the dish I'm cooking. I figured almost all the *khoresht* (stews) I make fall into yellow, green or red categories. So here are my spice mixes for each:

GREEN ADVIEH
For 'green' *khoresht* such as Khoreshteh Esfenaj (page 92), Ghormeh Sabzi (page 186)

2 tbsp turmeric

1 tsp Omani lime powder

⅓ tsp black pepper

½ tsp nutmeg

YELLOW ADVIEH
For 'yellow' *khoresht* such as Khoreshteh Morgh va Porteghal (page 62)

2 tbsp turmeric

1 tsp ground saffron

2 tbsp ground cinnamon

⅓ tsp white pepper

RED ADVIEH
For 'red' *khoresht* such as Gheymeh Nessar (page 212), Khoreshteh Ab Ghooreh o Bademjoon (page 48)

2 tbsp turmeric

1 tsp ground saffron

2 tbsp ground cinnamon

1 tsp Omani lime powder

⅓ tsp black pepper

ADVIEH FOR RICE
2 tbsp ground rose petals

1 tsp ground saffron

2 tbsp ground cinnamon

1 tbsp ground white cardamom seeds

SOUTHERN-STYLE ADVIEH
2 tbsp turmeric

1 tbsp ground green or white cardamom seeds

½ tsp black pepper

⅓ tsp cloves

1 tsp ground coriander seeds

⅓ tsp ground cumin seeds

1 tsp ground ginger

2 tbsp ground cinnamon

¼ tsp cayenne or chilli pepper (optional)

½ tsp ground saffron

Stuffing for quails (see overleaf): 'spiced' rice with rose petals, pistachios, saffron, barberries and dried cherries

بلد رچين تو پر (شکم پر)

BELDERCHINEH TOO POR
QUAILS STUFFED WITH ROSE PETALS

Iranians love stuffed food. From meats to fish, fruits to vegetables, the art of stuffing has been around for thousands of years. They use rice (never bread), along with fruits, nuts and vegetables. They also love stuffing pastries and the most famous savoury one is the *sambouseh*, a delicate parcel of meat and cinnamon, created in the Safavid royal kitchens and later adopted throughout the world as what we call samosas.

This recipe calls for quails, my grandfather's favourite bird. Poussins are a good substitute.

Preheat the oven to 200°C/400°F/Gas Mark 6 or 180°C/350°F/Gas Mark 4 if using poussins.

Make the stuffing. Fry the onion in the oil and butter; add the chopped garlic right before the onion turns translucent and a little golden. Add the turmeric, salt and pepper, stir for a minute then add the rice. Stir this mixture for another minute or two. Add the lemon zest and juice and chicken stock or water; cover, cook the mixture on a high heat for a minute or two then lower the heat and let it simmer for about 15 minutes. Add the rose petals and take the mixture off the heat and let it cool.

Now prepare the basting sauce by mixing together the orange juice, pomegranate molasses, lemon or lime juice, saffron liquid and butter or oil in a small pan. Warm up until just heated through.

Prepare the birds by washing and patting them dry. Then rub or brush the outside of the bird with some of the basting sauce.

Add the dried fruits, sugar and pistachios to the cooled rice.

Take a roasting pan and place a rack over it. Stuff the birds and either sew the ends closed or use half of an already squeezed lemon or lime, or an orange wedge, the skin side out, and gently press it into place. Rub a little salt and pepper and olive oil or melted butter on the skin of the birds, put them on the rack and roast them in the oven.

Pour the basting sauce over the birds after they've been in the oven for 10 minutes. Baste a little occasionally until the birds are beautiful and golden – 30–35 minutes for quail, 50–55 minutes for poussin.

Take out of the oven and allow them to rest for about 10 minutes. Place them in a pretty serving dish and scatter with fresh and dried rose petals and a few slivers of pistachios.

10 quails or poussins

For the stuffing:

1 large onion, grated

2 tbsp olive oil

2 tbsp butter

2 garlic cloves, finely chopped

¼ tsp turmeric

1½ tsp salt

¼ tsp white pepper

200g (7oz) 1 cup rice

zest and juice of ½ lemon

500ml (17fl oz) 2 cups unsalted chicken stock or water

3 tbsp dried rose petals

15g (½oz) ¼ cup dried barberries, washed, or use cranberries

25g (1oz) ¼ cup dried pitted cherries

2 tbsp sugar

25g (1oz) ¼ cup raw pistachios, ground or in slivers

For the basting sauce:

125ml (4fl oz) ½ cup orange juice

1 tbsp pomegranate molasses

3 tbsp lemon or lime juice

pinch of saffron threads, pounded then dissolved in 2 tbsp hot water

2 tbsp butter or oil

To roast:

salt and pepper

melted butter or olive oil

To serve:

fresh and dried rose petals

slivered pistachios

مربای گل سرخ

MORABAYEH GOLEH SORKH
ROSE-PETAL JAM

In ancient times, this famous jam was called *gol ghand*, which simply means flower and sugar. The heady concoction of petals will transport you straight to the famous Persian gardens where the air is filled with the scent of roses and the nightingales sing. Imagine starting your day by topping your breakfast toast with this beautiful jam, or spreading it on scones with some clotted cream at tea time? It can double up as a topping for ice cream or panna cotta too. Best to pick organic roses or those that haven't been sprayed with pesticides. And best of all are Damascus roses, which have small petals and are very fragrant (see page 211).

Cut away and discard the white base of the petals. Place the petals in a large bowl, cover with cold water and put in the fridge for about an hour. Drain the water and spread the petals to dry on paper towels. Rinse and dry the bowl, then start layering the petals with 225g (8oz) 1 cup sugar, making sure they are all sprinkled with it, cover with clingfilm and place in the fridge overnight or for up to 8 hours.

In a preserving pan, bring the remaining sugar and 250ml (8fl oz) 1 cup water to the boil. Add the lemon or lime juice and then the petal and sugar mixture. Bring it back to the boil and then simmer over a medium heat for about 15–20 minutes or 110°C/220°F on a sugar thermometer – or do the plate test (see page 38).

Add the rose water and bring it back up to 110°C/220°F, which will take very little time. You add the rose water at this late stage so that it doesn't lose its fragrance. Pour the jam into sterilised jars.

fresh rose petals, enough to fill 1.5 litres (2½ pints) 5 cups

675g (1lb 6oz) 3 cups sugar

2–3 tbsp lemon or lime juice

2 generous tbsp rose water

LUBIA POLO
FRESH GREEN BEANS, MEAT AND TOMATO RICE WITH CINNAMON

1 medium onion, chopped

3 tbsp olive oil

500g (1lb) lean lamb or beef, cut into 1cm (½in) cubes (or use ground lamb or beef)

salt and pepper

1 tsp turmeric

2 garlic cloves, finely chopped

2 tbsp tomato purée

4 medium tomatoes, grated

400g can tomatoes

1 tsp cinnamon, plus extra

300g (10oz) green beans, chopped into 1cm (½in) pieces

⅓ tsp saffron threads, pounded then dissolved in 2–3 tbsp hot water

1 tbsp butter or 1 extra tbsp oil

For the rice:

600g (1lb 3oz) 3 cups basmati rice

1½ tbsp natural yogurt

50–75g (2–3oz) ¼–⅓ cup melted butter, ghee or safflower oil, plus 1 tbsp extra

⅓ tsp saffron threads, pounded

When I was growing up, we ate this at least once a week. It's a homely dish but it also makes an appearance at dinner-party tables due to the nostalgia it evokes. It's easy to prepare and everyone loves it, from young to old. Tomatoes and green beans – which are a relatively new vegetable to Iran, brought over from the New World – and meat are a perfect combination, along with cinnamon-flavoured rice. It's fantastic served with yogurt and Sabzi Khordan (fresh herbs, page 132) or with *torshi* (pickles, page 84). The *taadig* (rice crust) can be made with slivers of potatoes instead of plain rice (see Persian Macaroni, page 159). I sometimes use ground beef for a quick family meal but small cubes of meat work best. However, you can easily make this dish without using any meat at all. It's a winner with kids every time.

Cook the rice following the first steps of the recipe for Polo Ba Taadig (perfect fluffy rice, page 106), up to draining and cooling.

In a large saucepan over a medium-high heat, sauté the onion in 2 tbsp oil for a minute or two then add the meat, a few twists of pepper, turmeric and garlic, and cook for about 5–7 minutes until golden and the meat is seared. Then add the tomato purée and stir for a minute or so to cook away the raw smell. Next add the grated tomatoes and stir. Add the canned tomatoes, some salt and pepper and 1 tsp of cinnamon. Lower the heat, cover and cook for about 40 minutes.

Sauté the beans in the remaining tablespoon of oil and 2 tbsp water for 5–7 minutes to remove the raw smell. Add the beans, 2 tsp salt and the saffron liquid to the meat, then cook for another 10 minutes or until most of the sauce has evaporated – otherwise your rice will become soggy when you make the finished dish. The meat is relatively tender but will cook further with the rice.

In a large pan, mix two ladlefuls of the rice with the yogurt, melted butter, saffron and 75ml (3fl oz) ⅓ cup water. Heat briskly then spread over the base of the pan. Start layering the rice with the meat and bean mixture in a sprinkling motion: add 2 large spoons of rice and then 1 spoonful of the meat mixture and so on, shaping it into a pyramid. Finish cooking by following the method for Polo Ba Taadig.

The Persian Rose Garden

Iranians have a special relationship with the rose. It is not only a Persian motif in art but also a popular image in poetry, where it symbolises perfection in beauty. The rose is the object of longing, adoration and admiration of the nightingale, who represents the poet or the lover singing his devotion. The symbolism is ongoing and dates back a thousand years.

The rose has been cultivated in the province of Faristan since 810BC. Faristan was the centre of production of rose water, exporting it all over the world and sending 30,000 bottles a year to the Caliph in Baghdad. It is said that the Damask rose (*Gol-e-Mohammadi*), a delicate bright pink flower, is Iranian in origin and not, as the name suggests, Syrian.

Today, roses are grown in Shiraz, Kerman and Golpayegan, but the most beautiful-smelling ones come from Kashan in the middle of the arid desert, where they are irrigated by ancient underground aqueducts fed with natural spring water. No pesticides are used, making them naturally organic.

The rose festival or the *Golabgiri* ceremony in Ghamsar, Kashan is a beautiful sight. Women in colourful traditional clothes pick the roses by hand, just before sunrise. They strip off the petals and put them to simmer with natural spring water in large copper pots over burning embers. Tons of petals are needed to produce rose water and even more to obtain its essential oil. This traditional method of extracting the oil and essence helps keep the fragrance intact.

A Persian garden goes hand in hand with roses. The word paradise comes from *pardiss* or *pardissan*, meaning a walled or enclosed space. The earliest surviving garden is that of Cyrus the Great at Pasargad – you can still see the outlines today. This geometric garden pioneered the *chahar bagh* paradise design, which was made up of four *chahar* (quadrants) divided by waterways or pathways. Built around 500BC, it was the template for all the subsequent gardens and the style was exported far and wide – to the Moorish gardens of Spain and to Indian palaces.

My grandmother Talat's roses were spectacular. She arranged them in vases all over the house: pink with red edges, sunny yellow, deep crimson red, orange turning into coral at the ends or pure crisp white. They lasted for days, opening up slowly, each day revealing a bit more beauty. Ever since I was a child, I've been comparing any rose I see to those from Iran. I've climbed fences, crossed roads, come to a screeching halt in my car to smell a rose growing out from someone's garden or wild on the roadside, all the while thinking to myself, maybe this one will smell like the roses at home. I gauge the air to see whether it has just rained or if the flower has had enough sun to have released its perfume. If you have been to Iran and smelled a Persian rose, you will know exactly what I was looking for. But then again you could just simply open a bottle of Persian rose water...

GHEYMEH NESSAR

STRIPS OF LAMB WITH BARBERRIES,
TOMATOES AND ROSE WATER

This is a classic dish from Ghazvin where part of my family is from. As the name suggests, it is similar to the tomato-based Gheymeh (meat stew with tomatoes, see page 214) but without the split peas and with the addition of rose water, pistachios and barberries. The combination of roses and meat makes it unique. It is sometimes served at weddings instead of Shirin Polo (sweet rice, page 56) and its layers of green, red and white make it stand out on the table. Scatter some dried rose petals on the finished dish or even some fresh rose petals around the serving plate for decoration.

Cook the rice following the recipe for Polo Ba Taadig (perfect fluffy rice, page 106), up to draining and cooling. Set aside.

Pick out any debris from the barberries. Soak them in a bowl of cold water for 5 minutes to remove any sand. Drain and set aside.

In a large frying pan sauté the lamb in 1 tbsp oil over a medium-high heat until golden; add the turmeric and stir for a minute then lift out the meat and set aside.

In the same pan, add another tbsp oil and sauté the onions until golden. Add the tomatoes, seared meat, pepper and the hot water. Cover and simmer for about 45–50 minutes, or until the meat is very tender. Add extra hot water if needed – the stew should have a lot of sauce. Add the salt and tomato purée halfway through cooking. Add the saffron liquid and rose water 5 minutes before cooking is done.

Meanwhile, over a medium heat sauté the barberries in a pan with the butter, saffron liquid and sugar until hot – about 5 minutes of frequent stirring and watching over, as they burn easily. Remove from the heat and put them on a plate so that they don't continue to cook.

Finish cooking the rice by following the rest of the method for Polo Ba Taadig. Add the almonds to the top of the rice while it is steaming, about 5–7 minutes before it finishes cooking.

To serve, layer the rice with the meat mixture on a platter. top with the barberries, slivered pistachios, steamed almonds and a scattering of dried rose petals.

For the rice:

600g (1lb 3oz) 3 cups basmati rice

2 tbsp sea salt

1½ tbsp natural yogurt

50–75g (2–3oz) ¼–⅓ cup melted butter, ghee or safflower oil, plus 1 tbsp extra

⅓ tsp saffron threads, pounded

For the meat:

400g (13oz) de-boned shoulder of lamb, cut into 5cm (2in) strips

2 tbsp oil

½ tsp turmeric

2 large onions, sliced thinly

4 tomatoes, grated or skinned and finely chopped

few twists of pepper

125ml (4fl oz) ½ cup hot water

1–½ tsp salt

2 tbsp tomato purée

½ tsp saffron threads, pounded then dissolved in 2–3 tbsp hot water

3 tbsp rose water

For the barberries:

75g (3oz) 1 cup dried barberries

1 tbsp butter

¼ tsp saffron threads, pounded then dissolved in 2–3 tbsp hot water

3 tbsp sugar

To serve:

3 tbsp slivered almonds

3 tbsp slivered pistachios

handful of dried rose petals

GHEYMEH

MEAT STEW WITH
TOMATOES, OMANI
LIMES AND SPLIT PEAS,
TOPPED WITH
FRIED POTATOES

2 tbsp safflower or any
tasteless oil, plus extra

1 large onion, cubed or chopped

500g (1lb) stewing beef or
de-boned leg of lamb, cubed

juice of 1 lemon

1–2 bones, any sort

100g (3½oz) butter, plus extra

2 garlic cloves, finely diced

½ tsp turmeric

175g (6oz) ¾ cup yellow
split peas

2 medium tomatoes,
skinned and chopped roughly

500ml (17fl oz) 2 cups hot
water

3–4 Omani limes

½ tsp cinnamon

2 medium tomatoes,
cut in half

1 tsp salt, plus pepper

½ tbsp tomato purée

½ tsp saffron threads,
pounded then dissolved in
2–3 tbsp hot water

For the fries:

4 large potatoes

oil, for frying

This dish is very popular. It's an uptown and downtown dish, served deep in the bazaars, all the way up to the wealthiest homes. A good *gheymeh* combines all the flavours of saffron, well-cooked meat, delicate split peas, dry Omani limes and tomatoes – topped with thin crispy potato fries. People will drive a long way for a good one. I've been told that one of the best is served in a dingy restaurant near the railway station in south Tehran.

My late grandmother requested this stew be served at her funeral. She gave very specific instructions: 'The meat has to be cut in small cubes and it must be lean; make sure there is plenty of saffron... don't crush the Omani limes otherwise it will become bitter...' and 'whatever you do, please don't cry at my funeral... Eat this and enjoy yourselves and remember me in good times.'

My version is a little lighter, with fresh tomatoes, lemon juice and lean meat. My good friend Elina Shaffy is a vegetarian, and simply makes *gheymeh* without meat.

In a cast-iron or non-stick pan, heat the oil over a medium-high heat and fry the onion for about 5 minutes, stirring, until translucent and lightly golden. Add the meat – don't overcook it, you just want it to be seared but raw in the middle. Add the lemon juice and let it sizzle.

Add the bones, butter, garlic and turmeric; sauté for a couple of minutes then add the split peas and stir for about 3–4 minutes.

Add the chopped tomatoes and let everything bubble away for 3–4 minutes. Add the hot water. Pierce the Omani limes with the tip of a knife so that they don't burst; add them with the cinnamon. Reduce the heat to medium-low, cover and cook for about 45 minutes.

Fry the halved tomatoes face down in a frying pan with a little butter and oil until lightly caramelised. You don't want them to cook through, just colour slightly. Season and stir the stew, add the tomato purée, then place the tomatoes on top and cook for another 45 minutes. Add the saffron liquid about 10 minutes before serving.

While the stew is cooking, make the fries. Cut the potatoes into cubes or matchsticks and fry them in enough oil until they are golden and very crisp. When the stew is ready, remove the bones, place the *gheymeh* in a serving dish, put the fries on top and serve with *kateh* (soft cooked rice, page 109).

TIP: Use 1½ tbsp red *advieh* (page 204) instead of individual spices.

HALIM
CREAMY LAMB
OR TURKEY PORRIDGE
WITH BUTTER AND
CINNAMON,
SPRINKLED WITH
SUGAR

1kg (2lb) shoulder of lamb, on the bone or any type of turkey meat

1 large onion, thinly sliced

½ tsp turmeric

1.8–2 litres (3–3½ pints) 7–8 cups hot water

200g (7oz) 1 cup chickpeas or butter beans, soaked overnight and drained

300g (10oz) jumbo oats or buckwheat flakes

½–1 tsp salt

white pepper, to taste

2 tbsp unsalted butter, cut up into tiny chunks

2 tbsp light brown sugar

2 tsp cinnamon

Persian Halim is pretty basic but tasty and comforting. It is a creamy porridge mixed with lamb (or turkey) and melted butter, and topped with crunchy sugar and a heady sprinkling of cinnamon. It's made in restaurants in great big cauldrons, where the cook stirs it to create a creamy slightly stretchy consistency. You can't actually distinguish the meat as it melts and shreds into a creamy mix. It is Persian comfort food – perfect after getting caught in one of Tehran's heavy snowstorms or after hours of driving on the cold sleek wet roads of the Alborz mountains. It is traditionally made with wheat or barley but oats are a great substitute as they reduce the cooking time considerably.

Take a large pot and add the meat, onion and turmeric. Pour in the hot water, making sure it covers the meat, and bring to the boil, skimming any froth forming on the top. Cover, lower the heat and let it simmer for about 1½–1¾ hours, stirring occasionally. Add the soaked chickpeas or beans and cook for another hour.

Remove the meat and take it off the bone. Remove the beans and purée the meat and beans in food processor until smooth. Return the mixture to the pot, add the oats or buckwheat and cook for another 10–15 minutes, stirring continuously until you get a stretchy porridge. Add more water if necessary and check the seasoning.

Place in a serving bowl, add the pieces of butter (which will melt in the heat and create little golden pools), brown sugar and cinnamon. You can be creative and make designs on it if you like.

TIP: You can make this recipe with gluten-free buckwheat flakes. Soak them first in 900ml (1½ pints) 3½ cups whole milk or rice milk for 30 minutes before using. Halim is traditionally made with veal not lamb. I made it this way simply because I can't bear to eat veal. But the choice is yours: these days you can buy responsibly reared veal from some supermarkets.

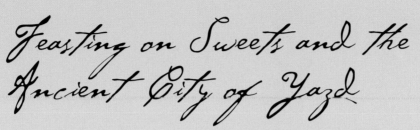

Feasting on Sweets and the Ancient City of Yazd

In the city of Yazd all the houses are made of mud. It reminds me very much of Santa Fe in New Mexico with its terracotta façades. The city has an air of complete calm, whether you are in a quiet neighbourhood or in the middle of a bustling bazaar. It's like a maze: in the narrow streets you occasionally bump into a local who offers you a sweet warm smile or some hot bread they have just bought. The streets are called *ashti konoons* or 'make up' streets; if you were in a fight with someone here, you would have to make up, as the only way out is to squeeze past each other!

In these passageways you see great big beautifully carved wooden or metal doors that open into people's homes. It's hard to believe that there are families living inside these immaculately kept ancient buildings. If you are lucky enough to be welcomed inside, you enter a hall that leads directly into an outdoor courtyard filled with flowers that has a small fountain in the middle with seats all around. You will notice the house's tall wind tower, its ingenious design channelling cool air into the home in summer and warm air in winter.

Yazd is the birthplace of the Zoroastrian religion, founded by Zoroaster in the sixth century BC. You sometimes come across monuments and beautiful palaces dating back thousands of years and no tourists in sight. Just an old man sitting at the entrance to greet you and hand you a ticket to your own private museum.

One of Iran's most famous sweet shops is in Yazd. I remember going there and being hit by the smell of saffron, orange blossom and roasted nuts. The family-owned store has pictures adorning the entrance of the many generations of owners. Here, experienced old men with thick moustaches delicately weave Persian fairy floss, roll mini *ghotab* (stuffed sweetmeats) in icing sugar, pour saffron-and-rose-water syrup over giant trays of *baghlava* fresh from the ovens and spread hot melted nougat with pistachios to harden before packing it in boxes. The boxes themselves are works of art, made from forged metal with paisley designs.

Before sweets were sold in shops, women got together and baked. My grandmother's baking sessions for *Norooz* (Persian New Year) would last up to a week. The women rolled out dough for *baghlava* (page 202), crushed pistachios and cut out Noon Nokhodchi (chickpea shortbreads, page 74). They chatted and baked, then every night they placed the day's sweets in the *ambari* (store room), putting them on enormous copper trays hung from the ceiling so that they did not touch the ground. Then her three little rascals sneaked down later to have a feast of their own. Yet my mum, aunt and uncle still say how deprived they were of sweets as children!

FAMILY MEMOIR

DAMPOKHTAK

YELLOW FAVA BEANS WITH
ONIONS, RICE AND LOTS
OF BUTTER AND TURMERIC

3 large onions, sliced thinly

100g (3½oz) butter or oil

2 tbsp turmeric

1 cup dried yellow fava beans, or butter beans, soaked overnight or for at least 2 hours

600g (1lb 3oz) 3 cups rice

1½ tsp salt

½ tsp pepper

750ml (1¼ pints) 3 cups unsalted chicken stock or water

⅓ tsp saffron threads, pounded then dissolved in 2-3 tbsp hot water

Dampokhtak means to 'air cook' in Persian – that is, the pan is tightly sealed so that no steam can escape and the food cooks to perfection. The method was later taken to India and Pakistan by the Moguls and now has many different variations there.

This recipe was given to me by my lovely angelic Auntie Maryam – some say she has my Uncle Darvish's spirit. I've adjusted the recipe as she is nicknamed Mrs Shoor o Kareh (Mrs Salt and Butter) by her kids, for her liberal use of these ingredients.

The trick to a good Dampokhtak is the beans. In Middle Eastern stores look for small, long, yellow dried fava beans – avoid the larger variety. It can be served with either cool natural yogurt or *torshi* (pickles, page 84) and Sabzi Khordan (fresh herbs, page 132) or just a crisp salad, topped with fried egg.

Fry the onions in the butter or oil until just golden. Add the turmeric and stir. Add the beans, rice, salt and pepper. Stir for a couple of minutes then add the water or unsalted chicken stock and saffron liquid. Bring to the boil, and boil for 10 minutes, then cover, reduce the heat and let it cook. Once all the water has evaporated – about 10 minutes or so – wrap the lid with a clean cloth or a couple of paper towels and let it cook on the very lowest heat for about an hour or until the rice is cooked and the beans are tender.

BIBLIOGRAPHY

A Mirror Garden, Monir Shahroudy Farmanfarmian and Zara Houshmand, Knopf Publishing; *A New Book of Middle Eastern Food*, Claudia Roden, Penguin; *A Taste of Thyme: Culinary Cultures of the Middle East*, editors Sami Zubaida and Richard Tapper, Tauris Parke 1994 (see From the Caucasus to the roof of the world by Bert Fragner, Eating habits and cultural boundaries in Northern Iran, Christian Bromberger); *Borrowed Ideas; Persian Roots of Christian Traditions*, Ramona Shashaani, December 1999, Iran Chamber Society, www.iranchamber.com; *The Cambridge History of Iran: from Nadir Shah to the Islamic Republic*, William Bayne Fisher, Peter Avery, Gavin Hambly, Charles Melville, CUP; Essays from *Encyclopaedia Iranica* online (www.iranicaonline.org): *Gol-Ab*, Houshang Alam/*Dampokhtak*, Mohammad R. Ghanoonparvar/*Judaeo-Persian community*, Houman Sarshar/*Chelo Kabab*, Bazargan Zogra/*Norooz Iranian Calendar*, Simone Cristoforetti/*Pre-Islamic Norooz*, Mary Boyce/*Rice*, Marcel Bazin, Christian Bromberger, Daniel Balland, Sogra Bazargan/*Sheep*, Jean-Pierre Digard/*Wine*, J. W. Clinton/*Zoroastrianism*, William W. Malandra; *The Essential Rumi*, translation by Coleman Barks with John Moyne, Castle Books US; *Food in History*, Reay Tannahill, Headline Book Publishing; *History of Food*, Maguelonne Toussaint-Samat, Wiley Blackwell; *History of Ice-Cream (Bastani) in Iran*, Ahmad Jalali Farahani, Iran Chamber Society, www.iranchamber.com; The Foundation for the Advancement of Sephardic Studies and Culture FASSAC, www.sephardicstudies.org/iran.html; *Iranian Marriage Ceremony, Its History & Symbolism*, Massoume Price, December 2001, Iran Chamber Society, www.iranchamber.com; *The Last Sturgeon*, Kristin Leutwyler, 15 June 1998, www.scientific american.com; *The Legendary Cuisine of Persia*, Margaret Shaida, Grub Street; *Le Monde Islamique: Essai de géographie religieuse*, Xavier de Planhol, Cornell University Press; *Narangi*, Guive Mirfendereski, December 2005, www.iranian.com; *Observations on prospects for further inland fisheries development in Iran*, Fisheries and Agriculture Department, Food and Agriculture Organization of the United Nations, www.fao.org; *Open Secret, Versions of Rumi*, John Moyne and Coleman Barks, Shambhala Publications; *The Oxford Companion to Food*, Alan Davidson et al, OUP; *Persia: containing a description of the country* [etc], Frederic Shoberl 1828, BiblioBazaar; *The Qanats of Iran*, H. E. Wulff, April 1968, www.scientificamerican.com; Unani healing systems, www.unani.com/comparison.htm; *Voyages du Chevalier Chardin en Perse et autres lieux de l'Orient*, Jean Chardin, ed. L. Langlès, IV, Paris, 1811; Wild and domestic animals of Iran, www.iranzoo.co.nr; *Yazd Pomegranate Collection*, Behzad Sharbabaki, 1997, Zamani et al 2007

Acknowledgements

A big thank you as always to my agent Louise Greenberg who made this book happen. Deep gratitude also to Francine Lawrence for sharing my passion about Persian food and culture, and for putting this whole project together. Thanks to Lisa Linder, my lovely talented photographer, Rashna Mody Clark for her delicate artistic eye and Sharon Amos, my editor, for her patience and understanding, particularly on the difficult Farsi words.

Much love and thank you to my talented mum, Mahshid Bazargani, the stylist for this book, who hunted down fabric and items from Iran so that the pictures would be authentically Persian, and who also cooked such wonderful food! This book would not have been the same without you. To my stepfather Rodman Bundy for his endless support. To my brother Reza Bundy... I wrote the stories with you by my side, even though you were on the other side of the world.

Warm thanks to all the other people who had a hand in this project, especially my cousin Lida Hariri, who painstakingly supplied the chapter and recipe titles in the beautiful Farsi fonts. And to my auntie Maryam Bazargani, auntie Vida Shahroudy and Dayi Hormoz Bazargani; my parents-in-law Jean and Roland Hughes; Faramarz Gharibian; Sam Gharibian; Foad Samiy; Mrs Simine Varasteh and dear friend Leila Varasteh; auntie Mahin Zarinpanjeh; cousin Mehdi Hariri; cousin Behzad Mohit (at whose home I became inspired to write this book); cousins Babak and Mariam Bazargani; cousin Farhad Mohit; cousin Maryam Ghajar; cousin Narges Kamkar Sharoudi; Nargess Hamzianpour; auntie Mahrokh Saadlou; cousin Shahriar Gharibi; Dokhi Adeli; Sukaina Kubba; Stephanie Mahmoud; Dora Levy-Mossanen; Mrs Mahboubeh Fakharian; and, most importantly, Zahra Khanoom and Roghieh Khanoom, who shared family stories and valuable recipes.

A humble note of deep appreciation and thanks to all Iranian women who pass these amazing recipes down to us and to the Iranian cookbook authors who have made it their mission to keep our culinary knowledge alive across the generations – your books kept us going when we could not call our mums, grandmothers or aunts.

To the spirit of my ancestors, notably my maternal grandparents, and my father, whose love of food was implanted in us. And to the new generation – my son Dara and cousins Soraya, Kamran, Kamand, Shereene and all the others – I hope this book will be the one you pick up when you want to cook for your future families.

Last and not least to my wonderful husband Paul: thank you for your patience and enormous help. This book would never have been finished without your support.

Special thanks to: Lida Hariri for designing and producing the Farsi fonts.
Ceramica Blue, London, www.ceramicablue.co.uk; Bloomingdales, The Dubai Mall, Downtown Burj Khalifa, Dubai, www1.bloomingdales.com; O'de Rose, al Wasl Road, Dubai, www.o-derose.com; Sarya, Hermes Art de la Table, Puiforcat, St Louis, Dubai Mall; Broadway Interiors, www.broadwayinteriors.com

Please note that when giving the recipe titles in Farsi, I've used a mixture of colloquial and formal language, just as we speak it at home.

Our Amoo Darvish – a source of inspiration

Uncle
Darvish